JAPANESE FINANCE
A guide to Banking in Japan

JAPANESE FINANCE
A Guide to Banking in Japan

Andreas R. Prindl
Morgan Guaranty Trust Company
of New York
and
Saudi International Bank

JOHN WILEY & SONS
Chichester · New York · Brisbane · Toronto

British Library Cataloguing in Publication Data:

Prindl, Andreas R.
  Japanese finance.
  1. Banks and banking—Japan
  I. Title
  332.1′1′0952   HG3321

  ISBN 0 471 09982 1

Printed in the United States of America

For **Roni, Kari and Chris**
who shared the Japanese experience

Acknowledgements

The following text, drawing on four years' experience as General Manager of a large foreign bank in Tokyo, is specifically designed for corporate finance managers assigned to Japan and for companies with subsidiaries or joint ventures there or about to create such entities. In trying also to give a deeper explanation for the rigidity of the Japanese banking system, hopefully it will prove of interest to other readers generally interested in having, like Theseus in Crete, a thread through the labyrinth of the Japanese markets. The theme is a broad and a rich one. To describe Japanese banking is to describe Japanese attitudes towards business and ultimately towards the outside world. An attempt has to be made to look at perceptions of the participants in the banking system and its users, skirting the edges of sociology and history. Many Japanese were kind enough to explain their view of the background of Japanese finance, as were several long-term Western residents of Japan. Without their help, this book would not have been possible.

The author would like to express his particular appreciation to three friends who have educated him about Japanese practices and read portions of the draft text. Father Robert Ballon, S.J., Director of the Socio-Economic Institute of Sophia University, Tokyo, has taught me much about Japan and pointed out academic sources. Richard W. Rabinowitz, Partner, Anderson, Mōri and Rabinowitz, spent many hours imparting his own outstanding knowledge of Japan's characteristics and approach to problems. Dr. Moneim El-Meligi of Rutgers University demonstrated ways of looking at perceptions and apparent values as a means of understanding the actions and reactions of Government officials. I have also been assisted by discussions with several practitioners: Toyoo Gyothen, Deputy Director-General, International Finance Bureau, Ministry of Finance; Kozo Yamamoto, Assistant Director, Banking Division, Banking Bureau, Ministry of Finance; Akira Nambara, now Manager, Okita Branch, Bank of Japan; Keigo Tatsumi, Senior Managing Director, Sanwa Bank; Atsushi Masuda, Director and General Manager, Nagoya Branch, Mitsubishi Bank; and Naoaki Kiriu, Vice President, Morgan Guaranty Trust Company. Kiriu-San helped me immensely throughout my stay.

None of these gentlemen is responsible for any errors; indeed, some may strongly disagree with certain of the conclusions made in the text.

The staff of Morgan Guaranty, Tokyo Office, have helped in more ways than can be listed: in patiently explaining much about Japan, in obtaining data and other material, and in accepting Western practices imposed upon them without demur, even when they may have seemed cockeyed in Japanese terms. Beyond that, the delightful atmosphere generated by this team—that of a family—made the writer's stay in Japan most enjoyable as well as instructive.

Mitsuko Hata, Tomoko Masuda and Miho Takeichi helped immensely in typing and re-typing several drafts in Japan, as did Heather Cutt and Penny Ralph in London. Nomura Research Institute provided many of the statistics.

Despite considerable assistance and encouragement from Morgan management and staff, the volume represents my own views and does not necessarily reflect the position of Morgan Guaranty Trust Company of New York or Saudi International Bank.

Lastly, I would like to thank my family for putting up with the irritations and absences caused by this effort and for supporting me in all I do.

Ditchling, Sussex   ANDREAS R. PRINDL
June, 1981

Contents

x

Introduction

This volume is designed to be a guide to the Japanese banking market and how to deal with it. The original impetus was to show the special problems which having subsidiaries in or borrowing from Japan may bring, and to suggest some solutions: ways in which techniques common in the West can be used in or adapted to Japanese conditions. Such an analysis was considered timely, as cash management and financial management practices available in Japan are not always known to Western companies, nor are traditions of bank and government relationships perfectly understood.

A guide to optimizing treasury management in a controlled economy necessarily examines the nature of the controls and the controllers. Rather than concentrating only on how to deal with the financial system, it must also analyse why the system is still rigid and the banking structure still fragmented in the 1980s. The text, therefore, considers the roles of the officials guiding the Japanese economy and its micro-sectors, down, in many cases, to individual loans by each bank. It includes the historical background of Japanese economic development in the Meiji restoration period of the 19th Century and reconstruction after the Second World War and a look at Japanese perceptions of their financial strength.

Depicting the state-controlled development of Japan in historical periods leads to obvious questions: why does the government continue to control tightly a robust economy which has become second largest in the free world only 35 years after World War II, as if it were still rebuilding? Why do government ministries try to guide a huge, chiefly open, maturing economy by minute direction more fitting to a small, closed and developing country? Why are market forces not generally allowed to set interest rates, or more importantly, to allocate credit nationally? Why are the Japanese capital markets not encouraged to become truly international?

Part of the answer to those questions may lie in the conviction of the Japanese of their own economic *fragility*, compared with the rest of the world. The most typical comment heard in Japanese conversations is, "We are a weak country with no natural resources. We have no oil, no coal, no minerals". The perceived need to protect this weak economy from a better-endowed outside world, or to export fiercely to pay for imports of raw materials, is all-pervasive.

A converse implication is that the Japanese may not perfectly assess their own strengths: their intelligence and flexibility, homogeneity, loyalty, respect for authority and obedience to law. These features are very like those of a family, a village, or a tribe and many commentators have remarked on such anthropological similarities. This nation-wide family, by not seeing its strengths, downplays thereby the role it could play in world affairs: in foreign policy, military alliance or financial matters. Japan is often called an economic giant, but a political dwarf. It is not yet a financial giant either, although there are many signs that it could obtain, and sustain, this role.

Other reasons suggest themselves, for example the national concentration on exports as a foundation of economic reconstruction and the need to supply capital-deficient industries with dependable and relatively low-cost sources of credit, aided by a high savings propensity. Institutional lag, i.e. the continuance of a financial structure and monetary control methods suited to the less mature economy of the past, is another plausible factor. A tendency to base the economy on cartels, and the interest in maintaining cartel arrangements by members of distinct banking groups can also be cited. All of these may contribute to the system which monetary authorities have traditionally used to monitor and direct the banking market.

The framework in which controls are exercised is used as a general structure for the following text, designed for the person who may enter into relationships with Japanese banks or negotiate with government officials. It attempts to combine areas of intellectual interest: how money flows, volumes and interest rates are set in a large, open market by government fiat, with practical concerns: how to use that market efficiently and how to tap its increasing availability of capital from abroad. It also calls for a recognition of Japanese strengths and an assumption of its rightful role in world finance.

Section I describes the regulatory environment, dealing with the two primary financial regulators: the Ministry of Finance and the Bank of Japan, the structure of the financial system, and the prospects for internationalising the yen, freeing the domestic financial market and allowing Tokyo to become a major world financial centre. Section II gives guidelines for using the system, whether to raise capital or to improve financial management of subsidiaries in Japan.

I

JAPANESE BANKING
AT A TURNING POINT

A Present Framework

CHAPTER 1

Historical Perspective

A book about Japanese banking is necessarily one which will describe a system of strict control by its regulatory authorities. Banking technology is roughly the same in industrialised countries; it concerns channelling the flow of funds from savers to investors, while promoting the other functions of money: use as a medium of exchange and as a store of value.[1] The monetary/banking system lies at the heart of any advanced economy, and its operations are too important to be left totally to market forces. Business investment and government financial needs influence official policy in this sector; if savings flows are too meagre or incorrectly allocated, monetary authorities will take action to augment or redirect them. Growth in money supply will affect the level of inflation, which government will also try to control.

The nature of those actions—the choice of which part of the technology to use—categorises monetary systems. In most Western economies, control over monetary developments is *indirect*, using market forces and mechanisms to regulate the growth of credit and money supply. An opposite method, not necessarily less efficient, is for government to allocate *directly* the flow of funds in an economy, the extension of credit by sector and the level of interest rates. This is often found in developing countries or those characterised by state socialism.

Japan has traditionally controlled its monetary system by direct state guidance and does so now, despite its advanced status as one of the world's richest economies. The tools used to channel savings flows, to regulate monetary volumes and to set interest rates are still direct ones. To explain why involves a look at Japan's pattern of economic development.

Many reasons have been given to explain Japan's remarkable economic success since it was forcibly opened to trade with the West in 1853. The reaction to that jolt, i.e. state direction of the economy, coupled with the homogeneity and intelligence of the Japanese, a high savings and investment rate, rapid infusions of Western ideas and technology have all been cited singly or together as factors behind Japan's rapid economic growth in the Meiji period and after World War II. Three of these diverse elements are useful as well in an analysis of the development of Japan's financial system: the Japanese perception of themselves as economically vulnerable, the role played by authority in Japanese society, and the success of state direction of other economic sectors.

A belief in vulnerability has pervaded Japanese thinking, both in the past and in the present. Japan has no substantial energy resources; it lacks essential. raw materials and fertile land is limited. For most of Japanese history, harsh conditions have kept living standards of the bulk of the population at low levels, although by the same token, strong, self-supporting community ties were developed in the characteristic rice-growing and fishing villages. These ties, like those of a family, have often been identified in Japanese national society as well. The feeling of fragility can lead directly to a sense of needing barriers or controls to withstand uncertain future events, whether political or economic.[2]

Perceived vulnerability and identification with a close-knit unit have permitted and, indeed, encouraged the development of authoritarian figures in Japanese political history. Central authority also has directed the use of limited natural assets and the energies of the Japanese towards maximum output, whether at national levels (historically through a medieval system of fiefdoms and tribute) or at the village level. At the lower level, that role was played in traditional Japan by the *cho-ro*, or village elders. In the Japanese rice-growing village, the allocation of water to individual paddies is the critical factor in the success of each farmer. Water distribution is decided by the village elders on the basis of benefit to the whole community, a community which is interlinked by the physical joining of the irrigation system to all fields in the village. Commenting on the social ties this system develops, Chie Nakane suggests: "This system certainly makes a village one distinct social and economic unit; without being a member of the village it is difficult to carry on wet rice cultivation. The fact that individual farming is directly linked with the village organisation, as appears in the network of the water flow, and the way in which households are inevitably bound to each other by water, determine the form of the village organisation: internally it involves severe economic and political competition among the households, and externally it presents the village as a tightly-knit organisation. The situation has been enhanced by the shortage of water".[3]

The role of the village elders in allocating a scarce resource in a tightly-knit society is exactly parallel to that of the monetary authorities in modern Japan and is used in this study to characterise their role of directing the financial system. Capital, like water, is a scarce resource and its allocation to specific uses shapes the economy of any country. In Japan, state allocation of flows in the financial system often interferes with uses which supply and demand factors might otherwise have determined. Competition between financial sectors is limited by government fiat. Flexibility can be reduced, as government direction is more blunt than subtle. Sophisticated financial instruments and fully competitive markets are typically not encouraged in such a structure; Chapter Four questions whether this system is flexible or efficient enough for modern Japan.

The analogy of water has external parallels as well. The Japanese capital markets represent a growing reservoir which increasingly can be tapped by borrowers in the rest of the world. A reservoir, of course, connotes a filling up and replenishing function as well as tapping. And it is the state of Japan's capital reservoir which will be taken into account by the guardians of the reservoir—Ministry of Finance and Bank of Japan officials in their roles as *cho-ro*. If use of that resource by local interests has lessened, owing to maturity of the Japanese economy, then more liquidity will be available to outside borrowers. If the reservoir—the Japanese money supply—is growing too rapidly, particularly from Balance of Payments surpluses, strenuous efforts will be made to recycle flows abroad. If Japanese capital markets are strained to meet domestic needs, the tap to outside borrowers will be lessened or turned off completely. Access to the reservoir, represented by credit extension through Japanese financial institutions, is directly controlled by Ministry of Finance instructions/guidance to those institutions.

That detailed state direction of an otherwise modern capitalist economy and its financial markets is not seriously contested, even when private financial institutions are negatively affected, relates in part to Japanese cohesion and sense of fragility. If an economic unit sees itself threatened by lack of resources or external competition, it will accept the direction of superior authority, whether coming from the village elders or from their national and societal counterparts. Although perhaps not sharing proportionately in allocation, the unit's continuing role in a more prosperous whole is implicitly guaranteed.

The tendency to accept authority is augmented by the visible success of state economic and financial direction in the two most dynamic periods of recent Japanese history: Meiji and post-World War II. Less motivation to contest state authority appears if past state guidance has demonstrably paralleled fast growth, in which all the population has shared. Western organisations in Japan have also not questioned Japanese ways of guiding or developing the financial system.

Origins of Japanese Banking

In the 17th century, Osaka was a large trading and commercial centre, equal in size and power to many European cities. A diverse merchant class arose, which was later to play a major role in the Meiji Restoration period. The Kansai area of southern Honshu, Japan's main island, became partly urbanised and appreciable economic growth appeared in the second half of the 1600s.

Credit institutions developed in parallel. Different types of credit were needed to go along with economic growth: to merchants to build inventory, to traders for settlement of inter-regional trade between Osaka and Tokyo and to farmers to anticipate rice harvest receipts.[4] Different types of lenders arose: money changers, merchant financiers and lenders to the nobility. The merchant financiers developed exchange and remittance services and even a foreign exchange market (trading currency between holders in gold-based Tokyo and silver-based Osaka); these houses became financial agents of the shogunate. A forward market for gold-silver deals paralleled financing of trade and commodity flows.

In the middle part of the 17th century, a number of merchant financiers had grown large enough to become characterised as banks, and in 1662, an official bank credit system in Osaka was authorised. Notes issued by its designated members began to circulate widely and to be accepted as money; the first of these, based on silver backing, had appeared as early as 1617. The biggest ten banks in Osaka grew into a "Bankers Association", which later acted as a central bank in its control over the new note issue. It is characteristic that the Osaka Bankers' Association was developed with government encouragement "to create channels for official control" of the money supply, a significant stage towards today's financial system.[5] State/bank co-operation, and state influence over the financial system, can be dated back three hundred years.

Meiji Restoration

Shortly after the West forced Japan's doors open, the tottering shogunate gave way to the Meiji Restoration (1868/1912). After being compelled to look at their own economic weakness compared to the West, Japanese leaders set national policy to catch up, in a campaign of emulation, adaptation, education and investment.

State planners instituted a wide range of manufacturing industry. If private capital was insufficient to found an iron foundry or a railway, state funds were made available and state employees seconded to run the new venture. Entrepreneurial talent was tapped from the former aristocratic and samurai class, many of whom became excellent industrial managers. By the end of the 19th century, Japan possessed—if sometimes in rudimentary form—heavy industry in almost all sectors. Although it is debatable whether economic growth in the Meiji period was stimulated from above, i.e. by nascent industry and trading groups, or from below, by agricultural and small industry, the role of state guidance and investment cannot be understated.

A major thrust of the Meiji planners was also to create a range of new banks for specific purposes. The architect of today's Japanese banking system and its specific divisions between specialised sorts of institutions was Prince Masayoshi Matsukata, Finance Minister during the late 19th century. He was responsible for the Banking Act of 1882, creating the Bank of Japan, and the formation of the Yokohama Specie Bank (now the Bank of Tokyo) in 1880 to be the foreign financial arm of the Japanese Government. The Industrial Bank of Japan (IBJ), designed to finance new industrial companies, was created in 1900. In the same period appeared the Long Term Credit Bank and various semi-governmental institutions such as the Agricultural Co-operative

Banks. These banks still exist and are among the dominant institutions in Japanese finance, along with the city banks; they continue their specialisations. While the new types of banks complemented commercial banks, such as Mitsui, which had long offered banking credit and services, they also formed specific partitions in Japanese financial markets. Specific banks were created for distinct purposes to help a fledgling economy, "supply leading" before credit demand developed.[6]

Other banks developed from entrepreneurial motives, some within industrial groups, serving financial needs of group members, then customers of the group. Their activity expanded into unrelated third party trade domestically and into international trade financing. Mitsubishi, Fuji, Sumitomo and Mitsui Banks became the core of the industrial groups known as *Zaibatsu:* "financial combines". Common to all banks, however, was a sense of helping the national purpose by financing industry and infrastructure.

Post-war Japan

This motivation was re-emphasised in the aftermath of World War II. Again, Japan had to build industry from nothing; again, it was government which shaped the direction of rebuilding and the channeling of finance. The motto used to stimulate a defeated population to rebuild was "export or die", a thought still likely to exist in the Japanese subconscious. Although Japanese banks lost their branches abroad and much of their substance, they were the beneficiaries of the currency reform imposed by the Occupation forces. The long-standing pattern of emphasis on capital investment rather than consumption reappeared; the growth of Japan's economy allowed a large percentage of savings to personal disposable income and ballooned the deposit base of commercial banks. Those connected with *Zaibatsu* groups were strengthened by and in return aided their array of related companies. Those used as semi-official arms of the government: Bank of Tokyo and the long-term banks continued their historic role and, through their bond-issuing ability, had sufficient resources to sustain that role.

Today's Structure

Japanese banking is still characterised by historical patterns: state guidance, delineation of separate banking groups to fulfill different functions and less than modern markets. The first two features can be described as *fiat* and *fragmentation;* the third is a consequence of a system dominated by monetary authorities' direct guidance of rates and credit volumes. A system based on past divisions is using past tools; but the Japanese banking section no longer has as its primary function the financing of a developing industrial base. The authorities in that country have shown little interest in moving away from historical patterns of structure and control. This is usual of bureaucracies: change comes slowly and financial change, possibly affecting the levels of national reserves, the financing of government debt or Balance of Payments flows, even more slowly. But deeper reasons must exist, among them Japan's appreciation of itself as a vulnerable nation. If its financial system is fully freed, and left open to possibly malevolent forces from abroad, so goes the argument, the fragile Japanese economy could be hurt. The impact—economic and financial—of the 1974 and 1979 oil shocks has done nothing to dispel such thinking. (Indeed, certain recent financial changes have been retrograde: the imposition of reserve requirements on funds taken from abroad or the reintroduction of direct credit controls per bank on yen lending in 1979.) Whether these perceptions are true and valid is of little importance. If the Japanese feel themselves weak and endangered, no amount of statistical proof of their strength will quickly change their approach to economic life.

A second reason may be the lagging behind of the institutional framework. Japan has demonstrably moved into advanced industrial status. But this can be characterised as "catch-up" growth, and perception of Japan's economic strength is recent.[7] Success has come quickly; appreciation of it is short-lived enough that many Japanese temper their belief in success by reflecting on the Depression years, or the bleak post-war period. Importantly, the gentlemen who as young officials were guiding the Japanese economy through its post-war reconstruction are now its senior financial officials. Their own experience and training tend towards using the same monetary tools successfully implemented in a rebuilding economy, even if those tools appear to the outside observer as outdated.

NOTES

1. Henry C. and Mabel I. Wallich stress the point in "Banking and Finance in Japan", Chapter 4 of Hugh Patrick and Henry Rosovsky (eds.). *Asia's New Giant: How the Japanese Economy Works*, Washington: Brookings Institution, 1976.
2. The idea is echoed by a number of foreign observers, even being used in the titles of their studies, e.g. Z. Brezinski, *The Fragile Blossom*, or Frank Gibney, *Japan: the Fragile Superpower*.
3. Chie Nakane. *Kinship and Economic Organization in Rural Japan*, London: Athlone Press, 1967, p. 79.
4. See Sydney Crawcour. "The Development of a Credit System in 17th Century Japan", *Journal of Economic History*, XXI, No. 3, 1961, and Kozo Yamamura. "Towards a Re-examination of the Economic History of Tokugawa Japan, 1600–1867, *Journal of Economic History*, XXXIII, No. 3, 1973, for a fuller account.
5. Crawcour, op. cit., p. 3.
6. This observation is developed at more length in Hugh Patrick. "Japan, 1868–1914", in Rondo Cameron (ed.). *Banking in the Early Stages of Industrialization*, Oxford: OUP, 1967.
7. Thomas Pepper, Asia Pacific Director of the Hudson Institute sees the change from "catch-up" growth to "keep-up" growth in Japan as more important than societal factors. See: Herman Kahn and Thomas Pepper. *The Japanese Challenge: The Success and Failure of Economic Success*, Sydney: Harper and Row, 1979.

CHAPTER 2

The Market Regulators

MINISTRY OF FINANCE

The Ministry of Finance (MOF) exercises immense authority over Japanese business and financial life, and is chiefly responsible for Japan's financial interaction with the rest of the world. As the financial arm of the government, it is charged with controlling the spending of other Ministries and funding and resultant government budget. It oversees the financial system in all its aspects; the Bank of Japan works in concert with, but under the framework set by, the Ministry of Finance in carrying out national monetary policies. Banks and securities houses act under its direct guidance, whether or not this is specified in law. It is staffed by the most gifted graduates of the best universities. In their system, Ministry of Finance officials can truly be represented as *cho-ro* of the Japanese nation; like the decisions of the village elders sharing precious water resources, Ministry of Finance financial instructions are generally accepted as being beneficial for the nation as a whole.[1]

Duties

The Ministry of Finance is responsible for financial management policy of the Japanese central government, including budget preparation, tax structure and allocation of resources to Government agencies. It has responsibility for licensing, inspecting, guiding (and if necessary, negatively sanctioning) all Japanese financial institutions: banks, insurance companies and securities firms. As finance is at the heart of Japan's highly-leveraged economy, the Ministry of Finance has for many years enjoyed the highest reputation and power among Japanese ministries. For policy made at the national government level, the Ministry of Finance is the instrument to carry out the financial strategy underlying that policy, which it will itself help shape at formulation. Another way to characterise the Ministry of Finance is as the officer in charge of economic affairs of the Japanese Government. "Without MOF's agreement, it is virtually impossible to carry out any economic—or any other—policy measure involving government expenditure, regardless of the amount involved."[2]

9

Structure

To carry out its array of duties, the Ministry of Finance has evolved a structure based upon bureaux, each specialising in certain financial areas, as depicted in Figure 2.1.

The Minister of Finance and one Vice Minister are direct political appointments of the Prime Minister; they may or may not be finance experts. All other appointments are career Ministry of Finance officials, drawn from the pool of MOF knowledge and experience. Several faces are presented to the public; the Secretariat (and the Deputy Vice Minister thereof) is responsible for Diet negotiations, the Vice Minister-International for much of the dealings of Japan with international bodies such as the IMF, Group of Ten and the Bank for International Settlements.

Day-to-day decisions and control fall into the specific bureaux in charge of various areas. The bureau chief, his deputy and the section chiefs are given considerable authority to make operating decisions; most requests to carry out financial transactions, such as external loans, are submitted to and decided at this level. While foreign entities may have more contact with the Banking Bureau (if bank branches) or the International Finance Bureau (for capital transactions of all kinds), other internal bureaux wield great power. Traditionally, highest place is granted to the Budget Bureau, where intellectual and physical demands are intense. Second place in the hierarchy is commonly granted to the Tax Bureau, with Finance and Banking, then International Finance, considered to be next in authority.

But it is somewhat specious to rank the prestige of each bureau; each is paramount in its area of activity. The Finance Bureau, for example, decides the level of national bond issues, fiscal investment and loan programmes of the government, and directs the use of funds from the Postal Savings System. The Banking Bureau reviews all activities of domestic banks, including their foreign operations, new branches, new services, even pricing of individual transactions. It is essential to know which bureau to deal with, its principal officials and present policy in that sector of Japanese business before dealing with any issue.

Authority

The legal authority exercised by the Ministry of Finance comes from the government role invested in the Ministry of Finance as the financial arm of Japan and its specific requirement to prepare and monitor the budget. Each Ministry presents its own budget requests to the Ministry of Finance annually; while there are Budget Bureaux or the like in many other countries, they do not usually possess the additional power over the entire finance system, external financial affairs, social security and tax collection, which the Ministry of Finance does.

Further authority comes from the professionalism and expertise of the

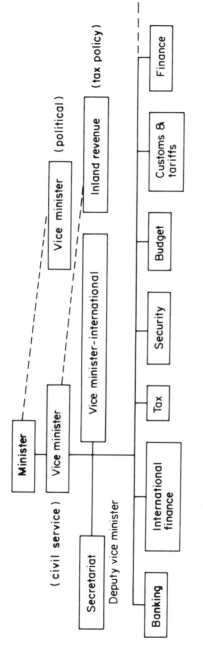

Figure 2.1. Structure of the Ministry of Finance

Ministry of Finance and from the individual brilliance of its officers. If it is accepted that Japan is a particularly cohesive society, and one which respects authority above all, then societal authority accrues to the Ministry of Finance through its guidance of the nation's economic well-being.

> "Standing at the centre of governmental activity, the Ministry of Finance and its Budget Bureau are legally responsible to the cabinet for preparing the annual budget; less formally, they are responsible to the nation for preserving Japan's financial solvency. If government spending is to be restrained, the job must be done here. Monopolization of the cutting role gives the ministry great power and appropriately high status; its officials are the elite of the elite, respected throughout the government."[3]

Societal authority derives if a ministry or group is perceived as a force adhering to and defending social mores and contributing to societal solidarity and well-being. Beyond the pure monetary implications of budgets and financial guidance lies a national belief that the Ministry of Finance, with the cabinet and other Ministries, is shaping, and should shape, Japanese society, as the *cho-ro* shape the harvests of a village. This common perception of its role, shared by people in and outside of the Ministry of Finance, adds to its societal authority. It is not surprising that many Prime Ministers come from the top echelon of the Ministry of Finance, nor that numerous ex-Ministry of Finance officials enter Parliament after retirement to carry out their societal role at different levels. The Ministry of Finance, therefore, is not only seen as law-enforcer, but also as the guardian of social order and cohesion in financial spheres. That the Japanese Government has been clearly successful in building and rebuilding the Japanese economy under great odds adds to popular belief in its wisdom, a belief which transcends a narrow legal construction of the Ministry of Finance's responsibilities.

Perception of its Role

Ministry of Finance officials admit to seeing their role as guiding the nation, controlling the economic environment and protecting the economy from unwelcome outside influence. Concomitant to such a perception is that little flexibility may be given to individual companies or banks; exceptions to specific guidelines will be given only after individual submission and deliberation. For example, if a company wishes to recapitalise its Japanese subsidiary with the proceeds of a Euro-yen borrowing, the Ministry of Finance officials concerned will take into account not only the narrow issue but also the broader issues of the Euro-yen market, the reserve role of the yen, the increase of the domestic money supply, etc. Protection of adverse influences upon the latter areas may preclude a favourable decision on the parochial issue of recapitalisation.

Limits on Authority

Despite its status as *primus inter pares* among Japanese ministries, limits to its authority define the boundaries of the Ministry of Finance's role. These include:

— The Prime Minister;
— Other ministries;
— Exogenous events; and
— The degree of acceptance of its guidance by the institutions it instructs.

The *Prime Minister*, in Japan's Parliamentary democracy, is both the leader of the ruling party and the top executive of the nation. As he leads the majority party, his legal, moral and coercive authority outweigh that of the Ministry of Finance. Despite the Ministry of Finance's shaping of government finances, the overall lines of the budget will first be set by the Prime Minister and his cabinet.

Other ministries and their duties can outweigh the men who hold the purse strings. Defence spending could become strategically important, overriding any other considerations, if the wrong combination of events in, say, the Korean Peninsula occurred. At times in Japanese history, military and domestic ministries have overshadowed financial concerns. The Ministry of International Trade and Industry (MITI) also sees itself as shaping the Japanese nation in industrial policy and economic growth and it would be specious to try to rank the influence of industry versus financial ministers on any one issue.

Exogenous forces, as shown by the long-lasting series of trade problems with the U.S. and the E.E.C., can sway or obviate Ministry of Finance policy. Pressure from other countries has often led to concession and compromise on the part of the Ministry of Finance. Speculation against the yen can hurt economic plans; oil price increases, for example, can wreck domestic price stability.

Very interesting is the degree to which the market guidance of the Ministry will be accepted. Traditionally, Ministry of Finance admonitions and instructions have been strictly followed by financial institutions in Japan. An increasing number of foreign institutions are operating in Tokyo; they are perhaps less prone to accept guidance not based on written law. Japanese bankers returning from foreign assignments may also be more inclined toward disagreement with the Ministry of Finance, particularly in areas where they feel both their narrow and Japan's larger interests will be served by liberalisation. However, inherent in the still general acceptance of Ministry of Finance guidance is an implicit understanding that the Ministry of Finance has also the responsibility to ensure the economic survival of Japanese banks under its aegis. Taking the *cho-ro* example again, the individual may gripe at and at first oppose the headmen's decisions. Yet, general acceptance of their authority carries with it the knowledge of and responsibility for the individual's own viability and rights. This concept, carried out nation-wide, reinforces the authority of the Ministry of Finance and its economic guidance, although a richer, more self-confident Japan in the future might see attenuation of Ministry of Finance authority.

Methods of Guidance

A variety of methods of guidance are found. For financial institutions seeking Ministry of Finance approvals, there are face-to-face meetings with officials of the section in charge of the area of request; verbal permissions or denials result. Regular meetings between the International Finance Bureau chief and the management of the main Japanese banks are held, at which broad explanations of MOF policy are given. At such meetings, there may be specific directives given to the banks, for example, to limit their overseas lending in yen or in dollars. Many of the decisions given are verbal, based on national economic or monetary policy rather than specific legal directives. The Ministry of Finance cannot legally stop certain transactions, e.g. the dollar lending of a New York branch, but it can use the full weight of its authority upon Tokyo management to assure that the New York branch will act within bounds acceptable to the Ministry of Finance.

BANK OF JAPAN

Second in the constellation of financial regulators in Japan is its central bank, the Bank of Japan, a product of the Meiji Restoration. Of the financial institutions developed after 1868, some were created directly by Prince Matsukata, others by merchant groups. While formed to assist economic development, such banks as IBJ and the Yokohama Specie Bank had at first little ability to fund the wide range and scale of new industrial projects. The Government was over-extended in its development commitments, and issued inconvertible Government notes to finance Japan's growth in its early stages. In 1872, national banks were created, which could issue their own notes; this added to a rapid growth of money supply, and in the late 1870s, to rapid inflation. In 1882, the Bank of Japan Act was passed to create a government institution of more stability, with the power to issue bank notes convertible to specie. The Bank of Japan thus began as a deliberate government creation, in contrast to the Bank of England, founded three hundred years ago as a public company.

Duties

The Bank of Japan (BOJ) is the sole note issuer, the Government's bank, the source of last resort of the commercial banking community and the implementor of monetary policy. It remains governed by the Bank of Japan Law, dating in its present form from 1942.

The Bank of Japan is firstly the financial arm of the Government, through which Government finance is channelled and deposits are maintained. Its second objective is to regulate the monetary system through an array of tools, mainly direct instructions.

A third major element of the Bank of Japan's role is bond market control. In the past few years, Japan has moved from a position of little national debt to a series of large central government deficits. The bond market in Japan was not able to absorb the new issues of Government bonds, although commercial banks were instructed by the BOJ to underwrite major portions. Fourthly, the BOJ defends the value of the domestic currency by its intervention in exchange markets to stabilise the spot rate of the yen.

Structure

The Bank of Japan is governed by a Policy Board, whose authority covers "all principal monetary policy instruments, including lending policy, market operations and the reserve requirements, and changing of the maximum interest rates of private financial institutions."[4] This Policy Board has seven members; the Governor of the Bank is the only internal member. The BOJ's internal structure is shown in Figure 2.2.

Important to note here is again the importance of each specialised section or department, akin to bureaux/sections of the Ministry of Finance. Commercial banks will deal primarily with the Business Department. From time to time, they will be inspected by the Supervisory Department. Foreign exchange transactions are reported separately to the Foreign Exchange Department, which sets open position limits. Policy is carried out and elucidated at these levels, where individual officials interpret and direct policy. Day-to-day contacts will thus be with specific sections, as with the MOF.

Authority

The Bank of Japan shares with the Ministry of Finance authority of the highest degree, although its legal powers are somewhat more limited. Article 42 of the Bank of Japan Law states that the BOJ is "under the supervision of the competent Minister [of Finance]"; Article 43 gives the Minister of Finance full power to "order the Bank to undertake any necessary business or order alternatives in the by-laws".

Its societal authority is high; Governors of the Bank are accorded great respect as the top professionals in their field, much like the Governors of the

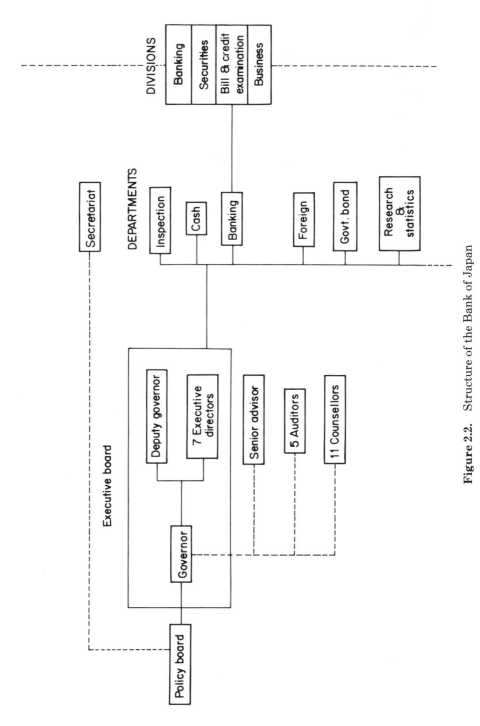

Figure 2.2. Structure of the Bank of Japan

Bank of England. The Governor is appointed by the Prime Minister, but invariably comes from the top professional echelons of the Bank itself or the Ministry of Finance. This authority, as with the MOF, assists the Bank to guide the monetary system by instruction without specific legal powers in every case. It, too, can draw on the finest young college graduates each year to form its future officer cadre.

Perception of its Role

Bank of Japan officials raise serious objections to the view that the Ministry of Finance is the prime maker of financial policy. Their own publication states: "in practice, active mutual contacts and co-operation are always maintained between the Bank of Japan and the government authorities with regard to the actual business and policy operations of the Bank, and this power to issue orders with regard to the Bank's business has never been invoked."[5] The outside observer, however, would conclude that the Ministry of Finance is the ultimate policy maker as regards the economy, supply and demand of funds in the financial system and external financial transactions. (Some implicit proof of that dominance is seen in the steady complaints of Japanese bankers abroad: they feel themselves constantly hamstrung by MOF policies, no matter where they operate, whereas BOJ directives, more domestic in scope, are not often cited as a problem in foreign locations.)

Bank of Japan officials see themselves as promoting the economy in direct, technical ways: stabilising the money supply and financial conditions, smoothing of friction between competitors for funds and promoting international co-operation. A strong element is guiding, even teaching, the banks BOJ controls as to Japan's greater concerns and the problems of integrating Japan more closely into the international economic community.

Boundaries of Bank of Japan activities include:
— Ministry of Finance;
— Political constraints;
— Outside economic events; and
— Scarcity of modern economic regulatory mechanisms, or limitations on their use.

Because of its ultimate control by the Ministry of Finance, the Bank of Japan can be seen to have smaller boundaries than the ministries. Political constraints: the need to keep interest rates down for non-economic considerations, or to force government bond sales when market absorption capacity is small, limit its activities. Outside economic events, speculation against the yen particularly, affect the role and efficacy of monetary policy. The limitation of monetary tools is a major factor, commented upon below.

Yet, the Bank of Japan is a major member of the international economic community and has a role which extends far beyond national boundaries. Japan is one of the three great economic engines of the free world, together with the U.S. and Germany. BOJ policies will help to throttle up, or down, that engine and are more critical, and more publicly analysed abroad, than the policies of, say, the Bank of France or the Banca d'Italia. Japan's membership in the IMF, in the Group of 10, its active and major role in bilateral swap arrangements, its intervention to bring about exchange market stability—all have resounding importance beyond the more parochial spheres of national financial policy.

The *officials* of the Bank of Japan are drawn from the top graduates of the top universities, and cosmopolitan attitudes pervade middle and top levels of the BOJ, arising from the constant international penetration of Japan and the posting of many staff members abroad. It is indicative that the present Governor is fluent in German and Italian, as well as English.

Monetary Tools Used

The reflective and responsive manner of the Bank of Japan comes from the way it shapes monetary policy. The most striking feature of its control is the use of guidance and direct measures, i.e. the way it chooses among the standard mechanisms available to influence the growth of monetary aggregates. These are:
— change in reserve ratios;
— bank rate adjustment;
— credit ceiling setting; and
— bank credit extension.

Reserve ratios have a legal basis in Japan, but have always been small for domestic liabilities. At the end of 1980, they stood as follows:

demand deposits	1.0 to 3.25%
time deposits	0.25 to 1.75%

Reserve ratios are not only low, but infrequently adjusted, and cannot be considered an important element in domestic monetary policy. For defence of the yen, however, the reserve requirement on non-resident-held, or "free" yen, has been a major weapon. Such deposits have had 100% reserve requirements at times when inward speculation was rampant.

Discount rate The Bank of Japan discount rate is the foundation of the interest structure of the whole system. Raising or lowering the discount rate, an act of the Policy Board, affects:
— the actual cost of borrowing from the Bank of Japan;
— the quoted "prime" rate of Japanese banks;
— other short-term money market rates: bill, call, repurchase transactions; and
— indirectly, the long-term "prime rate".

The level of interest rates has an inelastic relation to the demand for funds and is not as powerful a tool to control credit and monetary volumes as in the West, because bank credit replaces a large portion of equity capital in Japan, and there is less resultant pressure to pay out dividends or even to show high levels of profitability.[6] Corporations continue to borrow despite the level of interest. Indeed, the nature of the mutually supporting relationship between lenders and borrowers is that borrowers do not pay back the bulk of their debt when the economy slackens or rates rise.

Much more important are *quantitative* controls and guidance. These have their basis in the Japanese acceptance of authority without written rules, and in Article 25 of the Bank of Japan Law, giving the central bank broad, undefined powers to maintain and foster the credit system.

Rather than to change reserve ratios or to affect markets by sales or purchases of securities to change banks' reserve levels, the Bank of Japan can change its direct credit policy. Three types of borrowers are affected: city banks, security houses and brokers in the call and bill market.

The overborrowed city banks are dependent upon permanent BOJ credit to sustain the size of their overlent balance sheets, whereas the security and money market participants are enabled by central bank credit to carry their inventories.

Directly complementing the availability of central bank credit is the use of *credit ceilings*. At times of inflationary demand pressures, standard BOJ policy is to set quarterly limits on the credit extended by each banking unit. This guidance can be implied by simply requesting banks to hold back borrowing or by setting quotas of credit expansion. Credit ceilings—called *waku* in Japanese—are typically imposed by quarter and may continue for many quarters.

Window guidance (*madoguchishido*) overshadows the above triumvirate of bank rate, central bank credit and credit ceiling tools. The direction and nature of bank lending in Japan is shaped continuously by guidance of the relevant BOJ sections. Funds will be directed, following national economic and industrial policy, towards or away from specific industrial sectors. Areas of new technology will be encouraged: computers, electronics and telecommunications, for instance, as Japan moves further up the technological scale and toward higher value exports. Areas where Japan is becoming less competitive and where the local industry is being phased out (or allowed to fail) will be downgraded: textiles, non-ferrous metal smelting. Banks will be told not to support a sector, such as the trading houses, if they have been considered too speculative; even credit to a single company can be fostered or decreased by guidance.

Madoguchishido is perhaps the most distinctive feature of the way the Bank of Japan directs the financial system. It involves direct, usually daily, contact between the central bank and the commercial banks. BOJ scrutiny will include banks' overall lending, sectoral credit, individual rate setting by transaction in many cases, the make-up of funding liabilities and foreign currency positions. To undertake such detailed guidance of financial affairs involves a great deal of time and expense on both sides; it raises the issue whether direction by fiat can be as efficient as decision by market forces, now that Japan is a mature industrial state.

That State financial control has been remarkably effective in reconstructing Japan and directing finance to its core industries cannot be questioned. The success of Japan's steel, TV, ship-building and automobile exports must indicate the correctness of government policy to stress these sectors and the efficacy of the financial regulators in guiding the indirect flow of funds to such sectors in a country where equity infusions have been small.

From its daily supervision and discussions with all parties, the Bank of Japan is able to react rather quickly to adjust to changes. Bank rate setting must be agreed by the Policy Board (and in practice condoned by the Ministry of Finance and the Cabinet, a time-consuming process in any event and a very long one where political pressures oppose rate hikes). Through the window guidance mechanism, domestic banks can be told immediately to adjust their asset or liability positions, or by the MOF to change their foreign lending activity.

Rivalry with the Ministry of Finance sometimes is apparent. The same conflicts as may exist between, say, the Securities and the Banking Bureaux in the MOF can arise between the Securities Bureau and the central bank. A recent example was the case of corporate bonds issued by Japanese companies overseas. The MOF was thought to have given permission for certain corporations to issue unsecured bonds abroad, contrary to Japanese practice. The Bank of Japan was seen to oppose this change, as it would logically lead to demands to permit issuance of unsecured bonds at home. Other friction can arise in the areas of interest rate setting, in the strategies used to defend the yen or in the debate on liberalising money markets.

NOTES

1. There is a voluminous literature on the MOF and the Japanese Civil Service, which goes far beyond this brief characterisation. See Bibliography.
2. Ryutaro Komiya and Kozo Yamamoto. "The Officer in charge of Economic Affairs in the Japanese Government", a paper presented at the Conference on the Role of the Economist in the Government, Dubrovnik, Yugoslavia, March 1979.
3. Campbell, J.D. *Contemporary Japanese Budget Politics*, Berkeley, Calif., University of California Press, 1977, p. 43.
4. Bank of Japan. *The Bank of Japan: Its Organization and Monetary Policies*, Tokyo, 1973, p. 6.
5. *Op. cit.*, p. 7.
6. Yoshio Suzuki. *Money and Banking in Contemporary Japan*, New Haven: Yale University Press, 1980, p. 64 ff., stresses this feature of the Japanese financial structure.

CHAPTER 3

Structure of the Banking System

Shaped by the vicissitudes of Meiji restoration, depression, war and reconstruction, the Japanese banking system has taken on its own unique form. In
the last quarter of the 20th century, its structure is still fragmented into four
major types of banking groups, although the distinctions are becoming blurred
at the boundaries. Strong direction by the authorities continues, even if certain
liberalisation in domestic money markets has come; guidance of the financial
system remains detailed and direct, rather than indirect. This structure shapes
the way credit is negotiated and granted in such a system.[1]

BANKING SECTORS

While many countries have seen the consolidation of their banks into either
"universal" ones: undertaking most financial activities, including underwriting, or into two large groups: commercial and investment, Japan has the
following clearly delineated sectors:

Commercial banks   — city
                    — regional
                    — local
                    — foreign exchange specialised

Long-term banks
Trust banks
Postal savings bank
Semi-governmental institutions
Securities Houses

These are shown in Figure 3.1

City Banks

This group of 13 banks is the heart of short-term and trade finance in Japan.
The largest city banks, which are national in scope and have branches
throughout Japan, form the core of related industrial groups, still called *zaibatsu*. Before World War II, four colossi existed: the Mitsubishi, Sumitomo,

22

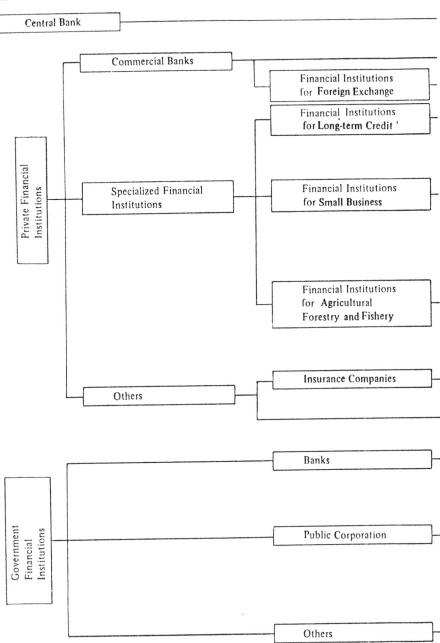

Central Bank

Private Financial Institutions

Commercial Banks

Financial Institutions for Foreign Exchange

Financial Institutions for Long-term Credit '

Specialized Financial Institutions

Financial Institutions for Small Business

Financial Institutions for Agricultural Forestry and Fishery

Others

Insurance Companies

Government Financial Institutions

Banks

Public Corporation

Others

Note: Figures in parentheses denote the number at the end of Dec. 1980.

Figure 3.1.   Financial institutions in Japan
Source: Bank of Japan

```
─────────── The Bank of Japan

        ┌─── City banks (13)
────┼─── Regional banks (63)
        └─── Foreign banks (64)
─────────── Specialized foreign exchange bank (1)

        ┌─── Long-term credit banks (3)
────┤
        └─── Trust banks (7)
        ┌─── Mutual loan and savings banks (71)
        ├─── National Federation of Credit Associations
        │         └─── Credit associations (461)
        ├─── National Federation of Credit Cooperatives
────┤         └─── Credit cooperatives (476) (Nov. '80)
        ├─── National Federation of Labor Credit Associations
        │         └─── Labor credit associations (47)
        └─── Shoko Chukin Bank  (Central Bank for Commercial and Industrial Cooperatives)
        ┌─── Norinchukin Bank (Central Cooperative Bank for Agriculture and Forestry)
        │         ├─── Credit federations of agricultural cooperatives (47)
        │         │         └─── Agricultural cooperatives (4,527) ( Dec. '79)
        │         ├─── Credit federations of fishery cooperatives (35)
        │         │         └─── Fishery cooperatives (1,760)
        │         └─── Federations of forestry cooperatives (46)
        │                   └─── Forestry cooperatives (2,015) (Mar. '79)
        └─── National Cooperative Insurance Federation of Agricultural Cooperatives
                  └─── Cooperative insurance federations of agricultural cooperatives (47)
        ┌─── Life insurance companies (21)
────┤
        └─── Non-life insurance companies (22)
        ┌─── Money market dealers (6)
────┼─── Securities finance corporations (3)
        └─── Securities companies (255)
             Housing loan companies (7)
        ┌─── Export-Import Bank of Japan
────┤
        └─── Japan Development Bank
        ┌─── People's Finance Corporation
        ├─── Small Business Finance Corporation
        ├─── Small Business Credit Insurance Corporation
        ├─── Medical Care Facilities Finance Corporation
────┼─── Environmental Sanitation Business Finance Corporation
        ├─── Agriculture, Forestry and Fishery Finance Corporation
        ├─── Housing Loan Corporation
        ├─── Hokkaido and Tohoku Development Corporation
        ├─── Local Public Enterprise Finance Corporation
        └─── Okinawa Development Finance Corporation
        ┌─── Overseas Economic Cooperation Fund
────┼─── Post offices ( 22,186) (Mar. '80)
        └─── Special accounts (4)
                  ├─── Trust Fund Bureau
                  └─── Industrial Investment Special Account, etc.
```

Fig. 3.1. (*Continued from previous page*)

Mitsui and Yasuda *zaibatsu*. Each contained a variety of manufacturing companies, a major city bank and a trading house. They became the core of the military-industrial complex which supported Japan's surprisingly long-lasting war effort. The *zaibatsu* were split up by the Allied victors after the war, but because of the rapid turnaround of U.S. policy towards helping and then needing Japan to industrialise as the Cold and Korean Wars began, the gradual rebuilding of the first three as "groups" was unopposed. (The Yasuda *zaibatsu* was more loosely reformed under the leadership of Fuji Bank—now called the Fuyo group). Other major banks—Dai-Ichi Kangyo and Sanwa—have similar groupings around them.

The role of the banks at the core of such groups and city banks in general is to provide short-term working capital and trade finance. The extension of credit which is never fully paid back leads them into the role of partner to enterprise and to "over-lent" positions. By having supported the growth of industry beyond resources available in the form of deposits and capital, money market and central bank borrowing becomes permanently embedded in these banks' liability structure.

Business reliance on external finance, a century-old tradition, has not been as much changed by the rapid growth and the profits of present-day Japan as might be expected. The pattern of high gearing, unacceptably high by normal Western standards, continues. Where loans from banks had averaged 68.6% of Japanese industrial companies' total capital in 1950, external sources, including trade payables, amounted to 68.7% of demand for funds by large corporations in FY 1979, although the bank portion was only 18.3% of total requirements.

There are a number of ways to look at this reliance on external debt in a country noted for its industrial development. First, this proportion is itself a direct corollary of the massive investment pattern of Japan since the war, the highest of any major country, as shown in Table 3.1.

Such an investment rate, coupled with abundant, flexible and disciplined labour, was critical in maintaining a growth pattern which allowed 10% real per annum growth for 20 years after the Korean War.

Table 3.1
Fixed Non-residential Business Investment as Percentage of Gross National Expenditures
(%)

Average	Japan	USA	UK	West Germany
1962/64	18.9	5.8	7.7	15.8
1965/69	17.6	6.7	8.0	14.7
1970/74	18.7	6.4	8.5	15.4
1975/79	16.9	6.7	8.5	13.7

1962/74 data taken from Shigito Tsurumi's *The Mainsprings of Japanese Economic Growth: A Turning Point?*, Atlantic Papers, March 1979. 1975/79 data collated from national statistics.

Second, the traditional pattern of national support for industry makes high debt-equity ratios considerably less risky than they appear on the surface. Firms of national importance have not been allowed to fail and bring about massive consequent default on debt. Rather, they will be in some way supported or at least amalgamated. The government agencies guiding and advising healthy industries continue their guidance in the case of disaster, while house banks support companies longer than is the case elsewhere.

Third, while the high degree of Japanese short-term indebtedness never fails to arouse comment, there is usually a tacit understanding that such loans will be rolled over at maturity; they represent much the same stability as long-term debt does in the West, although terms and conditions follow market trends. Both long- and short-term bank finance are also directly negotiated with house banks; debt issues are subject to government review and approval, and not allowed to endanger heavy government deficit financing needs by direct competition in the market place. Thus in 1979, domestic corporate bonds outstanding were only ¥3 trillion—less than 5% of total corporate finance sources—while bank borrowing of large-scale listed corporations was ¥55.8 trillion at 31st March, 1980.

Fourth, there is considerable undervaluation of assets in Japanese corporate balance sheets. Hidden reserves exist in fixed assets carried at cost, in securities carried at purchase price and so forth. Many properties are carried at their original post-war (and very low) cost. Debt-equity ratios to this extent may be overstated.

Cross-ownership is a fifth factor. Banks could hold up to 10% of the capital of an industrial, non-financial institution until 1980; this has been reduced to 5%. With many Mitsubishi companies, for example, each owning a certain percentage of each other, group cohesion and support is magnified. The banks also act as treasurers of their group. They undertake a high percentage of group trade finance and exchange transactions; they will also expect not to be paid off when clients are liquid and need less funds.

Foreign Exchange Specialised Bank

The Bank of Tokyo is the only example of this category. Formed in 1880 as the Yokohama Specie Bank, it was designed to be the external financial arm of Japan, a role it still in part plays. Before World War II, the Yokohama Specie Bank had branches throughout the world and worked closely with the Foreign Ministry in carrying out Japanese economic policy. After the war, it lost most of its branches (some permanently, as in Manchuria). Re-opened as the Bank of Tokyo (BOT), it is the only bank constituted under the Foreign Exchange Bank Law, which characterises its activity. The Bank of Tokyo has considerable influence in international matters and is a world leader in syndicated loans and private placements in a variety of currencies. Its branch network abroad has been reconstituted, BOT now having over one hundred foreign branches and representative offices, and its intelligence network is superb. The Bank of Tokyo acts in close harmony with the government and it is not unusual that an ex-Vice Minister of Finance is its president. BOT's role and its lack of a domestic deposit base are the cause of several additional special advantages: the ability to create yen from dollar swaps, a limit of 40% of capital to any one borrower, as opposed to 30% for the long-term banks and 20% for the city banks, and relatively higher borrowings from BOJ and the money markets.

Long-term Banks

The three *long-term banks* also have long acted as tools of government industrial policy. Their funding comes from bank debentures and long-term deposits; loans have traditionally been made to Japanese industry for plant expansion on a mortgage basis. Until a decade ago, the long-term banks were not deeply involved in international markets, but Japan's move to capital exporting and the maturing of its economy have forced them to move abroad, create foreign branches, and join or lead external syndicates. They are attempting to push towards shorter term lending domestically. In yen syndicates abroad, which are generally long-term and fixed rate, the long-term (and trust) banks have a natural advantage, since these deals, as well as domestic term loans, use the long-term prime as a basis. The seven *trust banks* fall roughly into the same category: they fund themselves with trust certificates sold to the public, basically akin to long-term deposits, and lend for industrial plant expansion.

All ten of the long-term institutions have tried to catch up with the city banks internationally; with the previous ability to create a foreign branch only once in three years, catching up has been slow. But all have large asset bases behind them and are improving rapidly in such professional areas as foreign exchange and international advice.

Postal Savings Bank

With assets of nearly $300 billion, the Japanese Postal Savings Bank (PSB) is the world's largest financial institution not directly acting as a central bank. The Postal Savings Bank has 22,000 offices throughout Japan, so that nobody is far from one. Added to the attractions of proximity are competitive interest rates and the absence of tax on interest on the first ¥3,000,000 of deposit. (Interestingly, the number of accounts of the Postal Savings Bank is over 200 million—about double the number of all living Japanese; tax-free interest has created a lot of dummy account holders.) Funds gathered from Postal Savings Bank accounts can only be used for direct public purposes. The Trust Fund Bureau which administers the Postal Savings Bank is empowered to invest

only in:
Government loans or bonds;
Local government bonds;
Government related institutions; and
Bank debentures.

The private banking sector complains about the unfair advantages, in rate and tax, given to the PSB, with some justification. The PSB also plays a role, usually an impeding one, in interest rate policy setting. Because of the political implications of disturbing the holders of postal savings accounts and the attractiveness of gathering funds for central government purposes through the PSB, its rate structure is not changed lightly. If rates are to be lowered, then account holders, particularly the farmers and small town dwellers who are the mainstay of the Liberal Democratic Party will be angered. If rates are raised, costs to the government are increased. The problems of resolving these conflicts can delay national interest rate decisions otherwise called for on economic or fiscal grounds.

Semi-governmental Institutions

A few large semi-governmental banks fall into another category. These are the agricultural co-operative banks, of which Norinchukin acts as the central institution, credit co-operatives and the like. They act as bankers to specific farming, forestry and fishing interests.

Securities Houses

Another important distinction in Japan is the delineation between commercial and investment banking, a separation designated by Article 65 of the Securities Transaction Law. This provision prohibits banks, trust banks and similar financial institutions from underwriting securities, as does the Glass-Steagall Act in the U.S., which it has emulated. (An exception is the underwriting of government and local bonds.)

Four securities houses dominate the market; another ten with them dominate the Securities Dealers Association. Not surprisingly, the major firms also follow closely the guidelines of the Ministry of Finance and the Bank of Japan. Issues involving foreign borrowers (Samurai bonds) or foreign purchasers will not be approved until the regulatory authorities have studied the national and Balance of Payments implications. (See Chapter 10.)

It is interesting to note the blurring of boundaries and heightened competition between the banks and the brokerage houses. The latter have also experienced a sharp foreign expansion, establishing important operations in the Euromarkets and underwriting a wide range of securities. The restrictions of Article 65 stop banks from direct competition at home, but their efforts to underwrite abroad are becoming more 'vigorous. Many banks have quasi-underwriting subsidiaries abroad, such as IBJ International Ltd. or Fuji International Finance Ltd. The latter was able to underwrite its parent company's FRN issue in 1978, a significant breakthrough and a portent for the future. On their part, the Japanese securities houses act as quasi-banks at home in short-term lending/investing transactions in the Gensaki markets, in private placement activity and financial services of all types. Abroad, the largest security houses are trying to enter the medium-term syndicated loan market in a managerial capacity, so that one may shortly see the brokerage houses acting as banks and the banks acting as underwriters in foreign markets.

SIZE AND FUNDING

The four classes of commercial, privately-owned banking include many banks of world size. Despite funding limitations of one kind or another, Japanese banks included 15 of the world's largest 60 at the end of 1979; members of all four classes of banks were represented.

Funding differs radically between the various sectors. Deposits are sought after, although fixed interest ceilings base competition more on service and other intangible factors. Much of Japan's high savings volume (still running at over 20% of disposable personal income) goes into the postal savings system or to the local and regional banks, which do not always have enough credit demand to utilise fully their deposits. These are then given to the traditionally over-lent city bank sector. City banks have further to turn to the Bank of Japan discount window and the bill market to make up the shortfall.

A major weakness of and irritation to the city banks is their inability to issue bonds as a source of funds. Only four banks—the three long-term banks and

Table 3.2
Position of Japanese Banks within World's Largest 60 Banks, 1979
($ billion)

Rank		B/S size
8	Dai-Ichi Kangyo Bank	73.3
13	Fuji Bank	63.6
14	Sumitomo Bank	61.9
15	Mitsubishi Bank	61.5
17	Sanwa Bank	60.0
20	Norinchukin Bank	52.5
21	Industrial Bank of Japan	51.5
22	Bank of Tokyo	50.8
36	Tokai Bank	43.0
37	Mitsui Bank	42.9
40	Long-Term Credit Bank of Japan	41.1
42	Taiyo Kobe Bank	39.3
49	Daiwa Bank	34.0
53	Mitsubishi Trust	32.9
57	Sumitomo Trust	31.4

Source: *The Banker*

Bank of Tokyo—may issue debentures in Japan. The long-term banks were given this special permission when the government was uncertain as to how well such banks could secure funds and to match the longer-term nature of their lending. Bank of Tokyo was granted the ability to issue bonds because of its lack of a large domestic branch network system and low deposit base.

Despite these justifications, the bond problem rankles greatly; issuing debentures is one of the chief goals of the Japanese city banks. The introduction of certificates of deposit (CDs) in 1979 went a small way towards meeting that demand, but the instrument was limited to 25% of a bank's capital, minimum denomination of ¥500 million and term of three or six months only, and no secondary market yet exists. The city banks are left to rely on the short-term deposits gathered by their branch networks. Even here, maximum deposit rates are set by the Bank of Japan (transmitted through the Bankers Federation) and there is no real competition for funds. The Postal Savings Bank deposit rates are set independently and are usually a little higher. While deposits of the city banks increase roughly in line with the economy, these institutions remain heavily reliant on the secondary market and on the Bank of Japan for funding.

The official discount rate at which banks borrow is the platform for all other short-term rates and attractive in terms of price, but the authority of the central bank over its permanent borrowers is pervasive. Since the Japanese system of bank control is a direct one of specific guidance and approval, the dependence of city banks on discount credit from the Bank of Japan fosters acceptance of that guidance.

BLURRING OF BOUNDARIES

Over time, the distinctions between the various commercial banking sections have also become blurred. City banks are joining long-term syndicates abroad while the long-term banks are moving towards shorter maturity loans. All four private bank sectors are developing their group branch network and offering a comprehensive and overlapping range of foreign exchange and money transfer services. All groups provide advisory functions. If two changes occur: debenture issues by city banks, and permission for commercial banks to underwrite security issues at home, then the historic distinctions between sectors will fall away. The fragmentation of Japanese banking seems inappropriate to many observers and the move to congeneric activities may further break down traditional boundaries.

CONGENERIC ACTIVITIES

The commercial banks are moving swiftly toward congeneric activities: consumer finance, leasing and factoring. Traditionally, Japanese banks have had a very low proportion of *consumer loans*. With a high propensity to save— itself a function of a retirement age increasingly remote from life expectancy and poor social security benefits—Japanese consumers did not traditionally borrow at the rate of their counterparts in the West. This pattern is slowly changing and a larger number of Japanese of all classes have begun to approach banks or consumer finance companies. The national branch networks and their local managers are beginning to re-gear solicitation towards this new asset area.

The field was formerly left to *sarakin*—salaried man loan companies—which lend to individuals unsecured. The bulk of these companies are quite small; many are scabrous. Interest may soar beyond both the point of legal usury (48% p.a.) or the absolute maximum level set by law (109% p.a.) Infiltration by the Japanese underworld—the *yakuza*—is evident, and strong-arm techniques are used to collect overdue payments. Often poor, afraid and beset housewife borrowers who do not know where to turn are driven to suicide as a result.

The impetus behind new moves towards consumer finance has come from two sources: the advent of foreign companies specialising in that area in Japan and the relatively weaker demand for credit by industrial concerns. Several U.S. companies—among them Household Finance and Beneficial Finance—were permitted to set up operations in Japan in the late 1970s. The permission from Ministry of Finance to do so originated from its desire to give a respectable alternative to the *sarakin* and to provide an object lesson for Japanese banks hesitating to enter this field. (The *cho-ro* here can be seen as introducing new ideas to stimulate local sources of credit.) The growth of foreign finance companies' assets and offices may have hastened the shift of Japanese banks towards lending to the consumer, rather than only seeking his deposits. While still small by Western standards, the average debt per household has risen from ￥131,000 in 1965 to ￥1,404,000 in 1978. Of total consumer debt of U.S. $165 billion at the end of 1978, $135 billion consisted of loans outstanding for house purchases, $30 billion for other types of consumer finance.[2]

The slowdown of industrial borrowing also stimulated the investment of city banks in other congeneric activities to broaden their range of services. These include *leasing* and *factoring* subsidies, often in joint venture form where the partner is a foreign company leading in its field. Credit card usage is also increasing; the major card firms are affiliated to banking groups.

FOREIGN EXPANSION

Another attempt to regain the dynamism of the earlier high growth period in a mature industrial state involves foreign expansion of all four types of bank. Japanese banks were not quick to build up a foreign network after World War II, although the biggest city banks did reopen their offices in New York and London in the 1950s (the Bank of Tokyo again was an exception, as its speciality was foreign trade and finance). Japanese banks in the post-war period concentrated on financing local manufacturing reconstruction and growth;

since this was financed largely by outside debt rather than equity or retained cash flows, there was neither impetus nor sufficient funding to support a second tier of foreign expansion. Japanese corporations were caught in the same syndrome; their own efforts were directed towards rebuilding and then expanding export markets.

The Ministry of Finance kept the brakes on foreign expansion of banks as well. Even in the late 1970s, when Japanese industrial and trading companies finally turned to direct foreign investment, Japanese banks were allowed to open only one representative office a year and a branch every three years. The banks were forced to watch domestic loan demand level off while their customers turned abroad to the large established worldwide networks of U.S., U.K. and other Western banks. When those banks also had foreign branches in Tokyo, Japanese corporate customers could be wooed away by cash management systems and sophisticated foreign exchange transactions.

WEAKNESS OF JAPANESE FOREIGN INVESTMENT

Some of the slowness in moving abroad can also be ascribed to the weakness of Japanese overseas investment by manufacturing and service companies. In fiscal 1978, Japanese overseas direct investment amounted to an all-time high of $4.6 billion, bringing accumulated total direct foreign investment by private enterprises to around $25 billion since World War II. This, in comparative terms, is still modest. Any one of a number of single U.S. companies may undertake fixed asset investment of around that amount in a given year. For example, Exxon's fixed asset investment in 1977 was $4.6 billion, or equal to Japan's. Several U.S. and European companies have fixed assets equal to the volume of *all* fixed assets of *all* Japanese manufacturing companies built up abroad since 1945. Again looking at Exxon, that company plans total investment—chiefly abroad—of $24 billion between 1978 and 1981.

Furthermore, Japanese direct investment can be divided into three roughly equal parts: services (trading and banking), resource development and manufacturing; the manufacturing portion of $8–9 billion is even more dramatically small than the overall picture.

Why has Japanese foreign investment been so limited? There are some obvious reasons. Firstly, there was the need to develop Japanese domestic infrastructure after the devastation of World War II. For nearly 20 years, Japanese planning, investment and strategy were directed towards rebuilding. Secondly, there was the history of Japanese overseas investments which were confiscated after World War II, which otherwise would have put the present total at a higher level. Thirdly, just at the point that Japanese domestic plant and infrastructure became well-developed in the early 1970s and overseas investment began picking up, the oil crisis brought chaotic effects to the Japanese economy and reversed thoughts of moving abroad.

Finally, one might stress a psychological factor: many Japanese companies are uncertain about controlling overseas subsidiaries 8,000 to 10,000 miles away and worried about such important questions as quality and cost controls in a multinational setting.

There is also a clear concern about the ability to manage non-Japanese and to be able to use the Japanese management and personnel practices which are so successful at home. Many Japanese companies have chosen the safer route of domestic rationalisation and strong emphasis on exports.

Three major factors are now contributing to the rapid growth of Japanese MNCs. Firstly, it is Japanese *national policy*—and of national importance—for Japanese companies to invest abroad.[3] Japan must create more invisible income in the form of interest and dividends in the years to come, as it cannot count upon ever-increasing exports abroad in light of the massive criticism it faces from America and the EEC. Unfortunate as it would be politically and inefficient as the economic implications are, it is clear that retaliation in the form of tariff walls and further quotas will be forthcoming if new massive waves of Japanese exports hit world markets again. By investing and manufacturing in those same markets and selling locally, such problems can be avoided.

Secondly, the world *wants* Japanese manufacturing in those markets. While Americans and Europeans become very irritable about perceived loss of jobs and closing of factories from Japanese competition, they are pleased to see new jobs created through Japanese investment. Over 81,300 jobs in the U.S. can already be attributed directly to Japanese operations there. Expenditures by Japanese companies result in an additional 261,600 jobs in America.[4]

Japanese foreign direct investment is just starting. If Japan moves as a nation from $25+ billion of OFDI to MITI's goal of $80+ billion in the mid-1980s, then the amount of jobs provided, business given to sub-contractors, expansion of local tax revenues—all positive factors, as seen by the host country—will increase geometrically. Japanese companies will soon realise, if they have not done so already, that Japanese practices and methods are *exportable*. Japanese can be successful in managing foreign workers, in producing high quality products abroad in less homogeneous countries, in marketing those same products throughout the world from a series of scattered bases.

Where house customers are becoming multinational, their house banks will not be far behind. As did American, then German and other European banks in their turn, Japanese banks are building up a widespread foreign network of branches, affiliates, joint ventures and representatives. The Ministry of Finance has recently relaxed its branching limitations so that city, trust and long-term banks can more quickly move into full branch status in many financial centres. Asset growth here—from financing local business and from providing Euro-currency credits—will likely outstrip local Japanese industrial credit expansion in the early 1980s.

The *cho-ro*, of course, do not relax their vigilance over these new foreign operations. Where there are Japanese bank branches, there is control by the Ministry of Finance and the Bank of Japan, either on the spot by direct representatives or their designates in embassies. Reporting back to the regulatory authorities in Tokyo continues in a minute form; Japanese banks are looked at worldwide, whether or not they consolidate foreign activity for accounting purposes. Financial companies abroad of the Japanese banks in, for example, Hong Kong, were formerly outside of strict supervision, but they appear to be caught increasingly in the Ministry of Finance's net.

NOTES

1. More detailed descriptions of the make-up of the banking system can be found in Bank of Japan. *The Japanese Financial System*, Tokyo, 1978, and Federation of Bankers Associations of Japan. *Banking System in Japan*, Tokyo, 1979.
2. *Mitsubishi Trust Report* "The Cash Loan (Sara-kin) Market in Japan", Tokyo, November, 1979.
3. Ministry of International Trade and Industry. *Japan's Industrial Structure—A Long-range Vision*, Tokyo, 1978.
4. Columbia University, Human Resources Project. "Economic Impact of the Japanese Business Community in the United States", November, 1979.

B Liberalisation

CHAPTER 4

Fusion and Freedom

THE INEFFICIENCY OF A FRAGMENTED SYSTEM

The division of Japanese banking into small distinct groups: 13 city banks, one foreign exchange bank, three long-term banks, seven trust banks etc. was described above. Historically, these groups drew on different sources of funds to sponsor different kinds of nascent industry. Trust banks were to accept long-term deposits and lend to support capital investment, the Yokohama Specie Bank to concentrate on foreign business, and so forth.

This system has become over-stratified. Japanese banks' assets are no longer as differentiated as before and there is considerable blurring of the distinction between lending sectors and maturities. The potential conflict between privately owned banks and government sponsored ones, particularly the Postal Savings Bank, has become accentuated, and it can be argued that inefficiency of allocation of financial resources has resulted. This can be seen in the following areas:

— Changed banking needs of borrowers;
— Duplication of services;
— Inadequate funding; and
— Low profitability.

Changed Banking Needs

The banking system in Japan is characterised "by specialization based on arbitrary distinctions between short-term and long-term capital, between types of money flows, and between the supposed end-uses of bank loans."[1] This distinction may have had validity in Meiji times, when all resources were being turned towards national development, and distinct classes of banks could be formed to stress particular types of development. After World War II, reconstruction strategy again used the specialised abilities of separate financial groups. Undue competition for scarce capital funds was avoided, trends to monopoly or oligopoly in part withstood.

Japan is no longer in a period of reconstruction, but of mature economic development. In the belief of many, it is about to become the first country to reach post-industrial status.[2] The original delineations of Prince Matsukata used to direct capital flows toward different areas of development are not appropriate to the 1980s. Adams and Hoshi, at the beginning of the 1970s, stated, "Even more remarkable than the quantitative growth of the economy has been the evolution of Japan's productive apparatus into one of the most advanced industrial systems of the world . . . but the financial system is basically the same which was organized for an economy which was struggling to get out of the postwar confusion."[3] When they wrote, the Japanese GNP was around $300 billion and few Japanese companies were on the list of Fortune's top 500 MNCs outside the U.S.A. In 1980, Japan's GNP exceeded $1.2 trillion; of Fortune's top 500 non-U.S. MNCs in 1979, 125 were Japanese.

The needs of such large, increasingly sophisticated enterprises are universal and it is inefficient and costly for them to deal with a plethora of different banks. The situation of the corporate borrower in Japan is rather like that of a prospective car buyer who must go to one shop for the body, another for the motor and to a third for wheels. Dealing with a smaller number of broader-based institutions, each of which offered a wider range of services and understood the full extent of the company's problems and needs, would promote better access to and use of funds.

Duplication of Services

Every major Japanese bank seemingly must have a research department, publish an economic newsletter (often in more than one language), entertain lavishly and compete for the newest and biggest headquarters in Tokyo. Each bank, whether city, trust, or long-term (somewhat less the Bank of Tokyo) attempts not only to offer its particular special services, but also to crowd into other spheres as well. Each bank of any size, for example, wants to have a network of foreign branches and representative offices. This in turn requires negotiating a probably inflated amount of funding sources in local currencies and Euro-dollars for those branches (such as issuing CDs which can surfeit the market for Japanese paper) and trying to outdo each other in facilities. To the outside observer, some of these foreign duplications are superfluous, unnecessary (are 24 Japanese banks needed in each financial centre?) and costly, as is the number of domestic branches throughout Japanese cities.

Inadequate Funding

With the blurring of distinctions between banking sectors have come problems of capital procurement. City banks, although moving into medium and long-term yen lending abroad (and expanding their long-term foreign currency lending), do not have term funding available domestically. Long-term banks are slipping into shorter-term lending, but cannot fund this appropriately.

There are several reasons why the authorities have not permitted city banks to issue local debentures, but the chief one appears to be maintaining the fiction of differentiated funding and services. Their lack of a true long-term base has kept city banks in an "over-loaned" position and at the mercy of the central bank, on whose funding they depend. Even the Association of Banking Institutions of Japan describes the parallel existence of city banks permanently short of funds with financial institutions permanently in surplus positions as "uneven distribution". To offset this unevenness requires direction by the Bank of Japan and funding through the short-term money market. Since certain of the costs (i.e. brokerage) of the money market could be saved, the division can be described as inefficient and unnecessary, if larger institutions had a more universal range of funding.

Low Profitability

Because of the need to meet changed loan demand in a period of slower economic growth, duplication of services and funding imbalances, Japanese banks show relatively lower rates of profitability than many Western counterparts. This may or may not be a test of efficiency—objections can be made to making any important conclusion from Japanese bank statements. Balance sheets, for example, are dressed up to show larger deposits and larger total footings at reporting dates; comparisons of income to balance sheets which are inflated for purposes of competitive ranking have little validity. Japanese banks, like Japanese companies, are less interested—as a generality—in absolute profitability *per se* than in other factors: comparative ranking, assistance to group companies, public esteem, relations with government. Japanese banking statements also have considerable hidden assets; land and buildings are carried at historical cost, which may be infinitesimal compared to today's value. Securities are usually carried at cost and large hidden profits are not brought into current income. Conversely, the banks' unique role in supporting the national government bond issues is often costly. In the six months to 30 September 1979, for example, the losses of the city banks from their national bond holdings are estimated to have run to ¥280 billion.

Table 4.1
After-tax return on Equity: Selected Banks Worldwide, 1979*

		%
Japan	Bank of Tokyo	7.85
	Top 4 city banks	6.37
	3 long-term banks	9.25
	3 largest trust banks	6.90
Foreign	4 UK clearers	16.41
	3 German universal banks	7.68
	Big 3 Swiss banks	6.57
	J. P. Morgan	15.2
	Citicorp	15.1

* Foreign banks—calendar 1979; Japanese banks—1 October 1978/30 September 1979.
Source: annual reports

Despite these countervailing factors, there is a case to be made that the artificial fragmentation and duplication of Japanese banking do not allow the same level of profitability as elsewhere. Table 4.1 gives some international comparisons.

ALLOCATION BY FIAT

The above section depicted ways in which fragmentation of the Japanese banking system may lead to inefficiency in allocation of resources. But there is a more fundamental, conceptual point here: can a central government in a large, open, modern economy direct capital flows by fiat? A central tenet of non-Marxist, Western economic theory is that free markets and forces of supply and demand under competition best allocate capital, over time, to optimum uses. The tightly-regulated financial system in existence in Japan is historically understandable, but increasingly divergent from the monetary systems in other countries of comparable levels of high social and economic development. When Japan was recovering from World War II, it was sufficient to allocate capital through direct guidance. But with a $1.2 trillion economy, mature industries and large amounts of capital now being generated by various forces, it is no longer possible efficiently to allocate capital and stipulate interest rates by fiat. Progress has been made in the money market sector, but the panoply of direct and indirect controls remains: overall credit ceilings per bank—which can be expanded to set limits on specific industries, disapproval of lending categories, such as to consumer finance houses—prescription of capital ratios, and innumerable other points of guidance.

This both fits the Japanese administrative mentality and the nature of monetary policy implementation. Given the degree to which directives will be accepted, it is not surprising that the financial system encapsulates this type of control. Such thinking is not typical of other OECD countries, although it is often found in LDCs with strong state planning. Central resource allocation by fiat is also a feature of socialist economics, whose own efficiency is highly questionable.

The regulatory authorities in Japan, in their defense, are forced in several ways to use a fiat system of credit control and allocation. Principally, they do not have available the array of modern monetary techniques available to, say, the U.S. Federal Reserve Board. Reserve requirements, while in existence, are small and rarely raised or lowered to affect the volume of credit extension. There is no Open Market Committee and no selling or buying of securities to affect reserve levels and interbank interest rates. Monetary policy is carried out, instead, by control over the specific credit extended by each bank (a cumbersome process) and direct, rather than indirect, setting of interest rates.

Given the present heavy debt component of central government budgets, it has been imperative for the Ministry of Finance to finance its deficits by national bond sales. In FY 1979, Japan's government sector deficit amounted to ￥15 trillion, in FY 1980 to ￥14 trillion. The commercial banking sector was forced to buy many of the ensuing bonds at issue price, although equivalent government bonds were selling at sharp discounts in the secondary markets. To help them refinance bond purchases, the Bank of Japan increases its loans outstanding to banks, particularly city banks. If strict guidance were not given to banks' credit extension, the bond flotation programme in this form would be obstructed.

Another political factor calling for government direction in the interest rate area is its financing through the Postal Savings Bank system. If interest rates on customer deposits were left to market forces, either the Postal Savings Bank's funds could diminish, or its interest costs increase, to the detriment of central government financing.

Lack of indirect techniques and political/budgetary factors cause direction of monetary policy in Japan to be carried out by direct intervention and rate and quota setting. The cost of government supervision is not insubstantial, given reporting requirements, daily telephone advice, frequent calling on BOJ for verbal reporting and long meetings with MOF for approvals of all types of deals. Inefficiency in banking results; government bureaucrats abound. And beyond these obvious costs comes back the conceptual problem: Can government really expect to allocate capital flows efficiently in Japan by its own directives? Do social goals and even prejudices enter the process? If *sarakin* are in disfavour, banks are told not to lend to that sector, although the development of decent consumer finance houses could well benefit Japan. If trading houses are considered to be too speculative, individual quotas per bank will be set to curtail their activities.

But such actions should really be the focus of legislation elsewhere, not carried out by bureaucratic policy. In several ways, to use domestic banks as social agents is to avoid the issue in national terms, to avoid legislative debate, to avoid the need to make a choice—escaping friction as is the Japanese wont. The same nuance arises when Japanese banks are told to refrain from certain foreign activities because of international criticism.

And, finally, is it likely that armies of bureaucrats can make better decisions by direction than can free markets? Despite their high education and status, is it likely that MOF/BOJ officials will be as efficient in guiding the financial flows as would the aggregation of individual firms in their profit-seeking roles?

FUSION AND FREER MARKETS

For these reasons, two major types of restructuring of the Japanese financial markets are due: freedom of interest rate setting/credit extension and fusion of the distinct banking sectors.

In interest rate setting, some progress has been made; the call money and bill markets are generally free of central bank interference, as are CD and *gensaki* rates. Full interest freedom would allow all liabilities, particularly time deposits, to have interest rates set by individual institutions, bringing more competition for funds (and better rates for the investor/saver). CD issuance would become unrestricted as to term and amount. Other freedoms would follow: extending loans without limitation to whichever sectors the bank wishes, up to internal limits or funding abilities. For this to happen, monetary policy in Japan will have to switch to indirect tools, a process which may be long in coming.

More immediately feasible would be to let *universal banks* develop in Japan and break down the artificial divisions of banking segments. Universal banks, offering a full range of bank loans, foreign exchange transactions and investment services, are typified by the large German and Swiss houses. These are formidable competition indeed, both at home and on the world scene. It is probable that they allow more efficiency than do Japan's fragmented banking sectors.

Creation of universal banks in Japan would force fusion of city and trust banks, creating a smaller number of much larger units with a full banking range. These units would likely incorporate their present congeneric activities: leasing, factoring, consumer lending, over time to become even more universal. There would be violent opposition from the securities sector if the banks would then be allowed to underwrite domestic issues, yet this would be a natural outgrowth of their status.

One source of present friction—the inability to issue debentures except by four banks—would disappear. Such universal banks would be permitted to issue all types of capital note or debt instrument, for any maturity and in any market.

BENEFITS TO JAPAN

Freer markets and freer banks should improve allocation of capital flows in Japan, increase efficiency in the banking system and enhance competition. On a national basis, the freedom of capitalist banking would better fit the status of Japanese industry. More mature, i.e. deeper and broader, capital markets would evolve. Duplication of banking facilities would be in part eliminated, thereby saving considerable costs.

There are dangers to this scheme, particularly in the oligopoly of giant banks which could result. Regional and local banks, less-skilled in comparison to the national banks, would be weakened. The semi-official agricultural and forestry co-operative banks would have a smaller role to play. The minor securities houses' profits would be further squeezed; even the large four would be adversely affected.

These problems can be solved by proper transition, as the benefits to Japan outweigh the negative implications. Above all, the strength of the Japanese banks *internationally* would increase logarithmically. It is not always realised that with greater size in banking comes greater competitive ability, arising from specialisation, creation of particular advisory teams, larger loan limits, and better research. Rather than maintaining 30 research teams and foreign exchange departments, a smaller number of world class economics and trading divisions could be created. The skills of a BOT, an IBJ, and a Mitsubishi Bank could be combined in single institutions, of which perhaps about one dozen would exist. The new institutions would assist the inflow of invisible income and be instrumental in developing a world finance centre in Tokyo, another change whose time has come.

It is interesting to consider why the development from fiat to market freedom and from fragmentation of the banking system to fusion has so far shown little sign of taking place. The probable inefficiencies and costs of the present system are well-known. The Wallichs' explanation is excellent: "What many Western observers have regarded as deficiencies—such as the tight control of interest rates, the absence of a bond market and the discriminatory allocation of resources in favour of a big manufacturing industry—were not the result of ignorance of, or inability to apply, different methods. In the pre-World War II period, Japan's interest rates moved more flexibly and the government tried to spread credit widely. The policy decision to depart temporarily from these practices was at least partly motivated by the exigencies of the post-war period."[4] Certainly, the Japanese stress on industrial development led to maintaining a controlled and docile financial community. Some bank participants may also prefer the present system, accepting limits and inefficiencies as the cost of ensuring that government will not let them fail. The system has worked admirably in the past in providing credit to industry in periods of rapid growth; growth rates may have slowed but the structure adapted to a different type of investment demand is lagging behind.

NOTES

1. L.S. Presnell, (ed). *Money and Banking in Japan*, London: Macmillan, 1973, p. xv.
2. For example, Herman Kahn. *The Emerging Japanese Superstate*, London: Pelican Books, 1973.
3. T.F.M. Adams and Iwao Hoshii. *A Financial History of the New Japan*, Tokyo: Kodansha, 1972, p. 164.
4. H.C. and M.I. Wallich. Ibid., p. 253.

CHAPTER 5

Internationalisation of the Yen

Given Japan's increasing international ties and penetration, another area to examine is the future role of the yen. Will it become "internationalised" and play a larger role in international finance, be the major element in a new yen bloc, or remain a local currency? To examine the possible outcome, a theoretical basis—definition of what the term "internationalisation" means—is necessary. After defining those elements which make a currency international, it is possible to identify how far Japan has moved in each area. The forces in and outside Japan which are working for and against such internationalisation in the early 1980s, can then perhaps be more clearly seen. Such is the subject of this chapter, which will conclude with analysis of probable trends of the yen's role, and with reasons why internationalisation of the yen is irreversible and inevitable.

The term "internationalisation" is often heard, but rarely explained. Inherent in the term "internationalisation" of a currency is its use outside of its own country. But does this mean each and any use of the currency, from being carried by tourists and exchanged abroad, to forming part of the international reserves of central governments? A currency used in a "bloc" must be an international one, by definition. But there is no yen bloc at present and currency areas or blocs have died or are dying out after colonialism has expired.

A currency is used at home as a medium of exchange and a store of value. This gives two readily definable parallels for the use of a currency abroad: invoicing and payment in international trade and holding as international reserves. Two more international uses are related: financing of trade, particularly, but not necessarily, when invoiced in the currency in question; and financing in general. However, internationalisation is less a specific situation than a process of moving into, or increasing penetration in, any of the above four areas.

(A fifth area is sometimes added, that of intervention. If a currency is used by central banks to support the value of a second currency, i.e., by intervening directly in the foreign exchange markets, then it is also playing an international role, and one which differs sharply from that of domestic money.)

Since movement into all these areas is necessary to constitute general internationalisation of a currency, then it is instructive to inspect, and project, how far these trends may go as regards the yen.

In *trade invoicing*, a steady trend towards using yen can be seen. Japan historically has invoiced its exports, and been invoiced for its imports, in currencies other than the yen, a unique situation for larger industrialised countries. In 1976, the proportion of exports denominated in the respective local currency was then 87% for West Germany, 73% for the U.K., 68% for France and over 90% for the U.S. The unusual situation in Japan has changed; the figure for 1979 was 24.9% and 1980 estimates indicate over 30% yen invoicing for exports from Japan.

A much smaller growth has been seen in invoicing of sales to Japan (i.e., its imports) in yen, a little surprising in the light of the strength of the yen in 1977/78 and its recovery after weakness in 1979/80. This gap is related to financing costs and financing availability, discussed below.

The yen has not been used in any noticeable way for invoicing of trade which does not cross Japanese borders, i.e., third country trade. This may well come; the attempts of Iran to invoice in and receive payment for crude sales in currencies other than the dollar during the 1979/80 hostage crisis are an example. While that example was political, in the future OPEC or other exporters may well include yen in their invoicing procedures, as a part of a more general diversification process away from the U.S. dollar.

Trade financing is also showing an increase in the use of yen finance, a movement towards the widely discussed *yen shift*. In its narrowest definition, the yen shift refers to the financing of imports—to a lesser degree of exports—in yen rather than foreign currencies. Traditionally, trade finance for Japanese imports and exports has been done in dollars, rather than yen; as the Japanese economy thrived and the yen strengthened in the late 1970s, the yen shift seemed to be right around the corner. The yen shift was publicly stated as government policy, particularly to reduce the dependence of Japanese banks on external dollar borrowings.

Four conditions must be present for a massive shift to yen trade finance to occur. Yen interest rates have to be the same or below traditional dollar financing costs. There must be sufficient availability of yen credit. Japan's external reserves have to be strong enough to weather the short-term possible impact of repayment of dollars previously borrowed to finance trade. Lastly, the yen must be seen by importers and exporters alike as having reached a medium-term plateau, above which it will not quickly or sharply rise.

The first three conditions were fulfilled in the late 1970s. Yen rates became much cheaper than dollars; import financing facilities made available by the Bank of Japan in 1978/79 through the Japanese banks cost importers about 6% less than uncovered dollar import financing. Local credit became readily available as most banks in the same period had difficulty in using their liquidity. Japan's announced reserves were among the largest in the OECD, sufficient to withstand the gradual repayment of Japanese trade-related dollar borrowings.

The possible strength of the yen remains a major obstacle to the yen shift and it acts in two ways. If the yen is perceived as having considerable short-term appreciation potential, then dollars, rather than yen, will be borrowed. Abetting this psychological influence is often the premium of the forward yen against the forward dollar. By borrowing dollars, selling them spot and buying them forward, Japanese importers can at times create yen funding for a net cost below any short-term yen loan rates in Japan. If the yen reaches a stable level, forward premia should move to interest parity levels and make the yen shift more likely.

Financing of a more general nature in yen is characterised by the advent of *samurai bonds* and *Euro-yen transactions*. The steady growth of the *Euro-yen* markets abroad signifies an important use of the yen by foreigners for financing or hedging. The Euro-yen deposit/loan market surpassed a level of $8 billion by early 1980. About half of this amount represented deposits in the European, chiefly London, branches of Japanese banks. Hong Kong and Singapore Euro-yen deposits are also growing rapidly in size.

This market is still rudimentary and imperfect. Quotes are not readily available for all maturities or large amounts. Rates may differ from swapped-in yen (thus providing an arbitrage opportunity for bankers in Tokyo).

The appeal of the Euro-yen market to deposit holders is that rates are not subject to official influence, as are those of yen held by non-residents in Tokyo and higher rates can sometimes be achieved. The deposit market offers a short-term lay-off possibility for borrowers of long-term yen in the form of bonds, loans or private placements which are not yet ready to use or convert the proceeds. There are no reserve requirements and (usually) no withholding tax. Therefore, the Euro-yen market offers the flexibility and universalism of other Euro-currency markets. For the borrower, there is ready availability, at times cheaper rates than dollars, and the chance to hedge yen receivables without borrowing from Tokyo. Euro-yen loans are made on a cost plus spread basis, without compensating balances and with a minimum of documentation. Although Tokyo banks at times have severe credit ceilings, none exist in the Euro-yen market. Its continued existence seems assured.

The fourth leg of internationalisation of the yen is the hardest to quantify, but undoubtedly the most worrisome to Japanese officialdom. The holding of yen in *international reserves* has been growing, from 0.6% in 1976 to over 4% in 1980. (Included in this amount is a recent large increase in central banks' holdings of Euro-yen and yen bonds.) Both Japan's trade partners and more distant central banks seeking diversification of their reserves have moved into holding new or more yen assets and some of the strength of the yen in late 1980 is a direct result. Being a reserve currency is a mixed blessing, as the British, Germans and Americans have come to realise. There are also physical limitations to this trend, in the still limited array of yen instruments in which to invest and the relative smallness of the Euro-yen market compared to other Euro-currencies.

But Japan is the free world's second biggest economy, it has many of the most vigorous and successful international companies and its growth rates should be at the high end of the range of OECD countries for the foreseeable future. Under these circumstances, it is unlikely that the trend towards holding more yen as international reserves will be stopped.

The final stage, intervention, has passed the yen by, since its traditionally small use abroad—and IMF practices—precluded its use for intervention. Only in isolated, hopefully unique cases of extreme speculative pressure has the yen been used to protect the dollar's value in the context of bilateral swap arrangements with the U.S. Federal Reserve.

There are four structural factors which one can identify as strongly aiding the yen's internationalisation. First, the massive trade and current account surpluses of Japan, which became acute in 1976/78, resulting in a large reserve build-up. Second, the situation in Japan of a secular excess of savings over investment, an excess which can be channelled abroad. Third, the growing international branch network and expertise of the Japanese banks, as well as the involvement of the foreign bank branches in Japan. Fourth, the strategic position of Tokyo as the natural financial centre in Asia, which on the basis of population, resources, and relative political stability is the fastest growing region in the world.

If internationalisation of a currency starts with trade invoicing and financing, then Japan's role as a major exporter of finished products and importer of raw materials allows ample opportunities for its own currency to develop into an international one, as did the trade of Britain, France and the U.S. earlier. Japan's typical trade and current account surpluses *per se* are structural and necessary; despite oil problems, Japan should regain a continual trade surplus in the 1980s. Its foreign trade will remain an important percentage of GNP, if not at European levels.

Perhaps even more importantly, there is now a long-term structural condition wherein domestic savings in Japan outweigh domestic investment needs. As shown in Chapter Three, the percentage of savings to private disposable income in Japan is extraordinary at over 20%, the highest ratio of any major country. But the Japanese investment cycle is at a cyclical nadir at the beginning of the 1980s and savings no longer flow automatically into plant and equipment at home.

Unless better use can be made of these savings, they may lie idle, causing a deflationary gap. More attractive to restore both domestic equilibrium (and external equilibrium when the current account is in surplus) is to use excess savings increasingly to fund capital outflows. This is again evidenced in the growth of samurai bond issues, yen syndicated loans and private placements.

The third structural support for the yen's internationalisation is the worldwide penetration and internationalisation of the Japanese banks themselves, as pointed out in several chapters of this text. These institutions have a growing number of foreign branches. Their expertise is expanding rapidly and they are urgently looking for new ways to deploy management skills and liquidity. As such, the Japanese city, long-term and trust banks will be a major factor in finding new uses and new users for the yen abroad.

The position of Japan in Asia will assist the yen's internationalisation as well. The influence of Japan in the rest of Asia, particularly Southeast Asia, grows daily. Indeed, some observers feel that the old "East Asian Co-prosperity Sphere" has been reconstituted again in a less controversial way. Given the high percentage of trade in both directions between Japan and its Asian neighbours and the dependence of the latter on Japan as a market, their yen usage should be expanded even more on a regional basis than elsewhere in the world. Although a yen bloc is unlikely to reappear, relationships in this group of countries will be dominated by Japanese influence and should increase the use of yen in all four international categories in the future.

Inhibiting Factors

Two factors inhibiting the internationalisation of the yen are the artificiality of Japanese capital markets and the fear of Japanese authorities of the effects on domestic economic policy. The former is disappearing with the success of attempts to liberalise interest rates. The latter concern does not apply to all areas of internationalisation, because the Japanese government would be pleased to see more yen invoicing and more yen trade finance to lessen the external dependence of this country on uncertain foreign financial markets. The authorities are also at least benevolently neutral towards the development of a controlled international yen capital market, as can be seen by their permission of samurai bonds and yen syndicated credits. But a currency can have useful roles in all three of these areas and not reach full internationalisation if it is not used, or allowed to be used, as a reserve currency. It is here—with justification—that the Japanese authorities appear to be strongly set against allowing the yen to play a reserve currency role, i.e., held in the reserve positions of other countries or to be used as an intervention currency. Officials in Tokyo have seen the problems which other countries have had, once their currency became widely held abroad, particularly from the effects of portfolio shifting by both private companies and central banks.

In the late 1960s, the German government faced precisely the problems of success which Japan had in the late 1970s: high external surpluses, appreciating currency and low inflation rates. The German government uttered many of the same arguments and used many of the same techniques which are commonly heard and seen in Japan today. Bonn tried from time to time to intervene in the exchange markets to hold the market down, but failed. Its attempt to erect exchange control walls to stop the inflow of money, for example, the "Bardepot", failed. Ultimately, the mark did become an international currency and a reserve one. This can be seen in its share of world exchange reserves, now estimated at over 7%, second only after the U.S. dollar, and in the approximately 17% D.M. share of international bonds floated between 1974/79. Yet the German mark continued to appreciate and the German economy, despite problems, to be strong. One cannot conclude that the D.M.'s movement into reserve currency status since about 1968 has been overly damaging. It is unlikely that the Japanese yen could soon grow to such a large share of world reserves and capital issues as to endanger seriously its domestic markets.

It is equally unlikely that the *cho-ro* of the Japanese nation can stop this trend. While foreign issues could be limited, the switch into yen reserve holdings is difficult to combat in the market place and even more difficult politically. As younger men move up in the Ministries, the authorities here may get over their fear of reserve currency status and allow the yen to grow over time into its rightful place in world economic relations, a place undoubtedly equal to that of the German mark. Such a development will run parallel to the growth of a dollar market in Tokyo, another type of internationalisation which is equally positive and desirable.

CHAPTER 6

Tokyo as a World Financial Centre

Japan presents a number of anomalies to the Western observer, but few as dramatic as the contrast between its economic size and strength and its self-limited role as a world, or even an Asian, financial centre. After 30 years of strong post-war economic growth, one could have expected Tokyo to grow into more of a world financial centre, a development which would also represent a significant threat to the more established centres in Singapore and Hong Kong. But the gradual liberalisation of the domestic money markets and exchange control as the 1970s turned into the 1980s, has not yet led to such a turning point in Japan's financial history. This chapter depicts the reasons why Japan is not yet an international centre and cites the problems Japanese planners will have to overcome—some in structure, some more deeply imbedded in the psychology already mentioned—before this can develop.

Visitors to Tokyo from abroad who look from the windows of their hotels and taxis would conclude that Tokyo already is such a financial centre, especially if they drive through Marunouchi with its scores of bank offices. Tokyo is indeed an enormous, vibrant and modern city with many banks, but it does not yet play the enormous, vibrant and modern role it could—and should—in international finance.

The term "world financial centre" implies that not only a country's own citizens are dealing in its local financial markets, but also foreigners, and for many varied purposes. Chief among these are trade financing, general finance in the form of term credit, syndicated loans and bond issues and investment of surplus funds. Such financial centres can be of two kinds: those where other currencies predominate, as in the dollar markets located in Hong Kong and Singapore, and those where the home currency is also used. Ideally, a world financial centre would include all types of financing and instruments and a range of currencies. London is even more an international centre after the demise of its own exchange control system, which frees sterling to be borrowed or transferred externally in both directions.

In Tokyo, only one of these areas—the use of yen by the rest of the world—shows changes and growth occuring. Dollar loans and other foreign currency transactions with non-residents effectively do not arise in Tokyo, although it will be argued later that these will evolve naturally over time, indeed that they should be strongly encouraged by the authorities.

Yen Bonds in Proportion

If international capital transactions in yen alone are counted, the size of these transactions does put Tokyo into world class status. In yen bonds, the Tokyo market has grown rapidly, as shown in Table 6.1, to stand fourth behind Euro-bonds, Zurich and Frankfurt.

Table 6.1
International Bond Issues by Currency
1976/79

| | % Share of International Bond Market | | | |
	1976	1977	1978	1979
U.S. dollar	60	55	37	41
Swiss franc	16	14	21	25
Yen	1	4	13	7
Deutsche mark	12	19	22	20

Source: Nomura Research Institute

Yen syndicated loans and private placements have also reached significant proportions. But there is a *"faucet"* aspect to the Japanese capital market. One can question whether a market which can be fully turned off by the authorities as a reaction to BOP trends represents an international one, or only a tool to offset unwanted flows of foreign currency in either direction. Yen lending potential is enormous, but not free enough to qualify as a world market. The internationalisation of the yen, particularly as it becomes a reserve currency status, will carry Tokyo in the same direction, but this area, too, is still resisted by the authorities.

Full World Status

World status will come only when the Japanese authorities lose their inhibitions about Tokyo becoming a dollar centre. Expanding into off-shore dollar deals would be a natural and timely development, involving the same institutions and often the same borrowers, and one which would bring benefits to Japan with none of the dangers of reserve currency status. Why have Hong Kong and Singapore taken over the role of Far East dollar centres, when the great economic engine of Asia is Japan and when the biggest international banks and multinationals in the region are almost exclusively Japanese? The answer lies in two simple, but critical differences: tax treatment and official attitudes.

The essence of an off-shore, or Euro-currency, market is that interest earned on deposits of non-residents is free of withholding tax, that reserve requirements are not imposed on such deposits and that "out-out" transactions, which do not touch the domestic economy, are not regulated.

Britain is a prime example of this, having captured the bulk of the Euro-currency market, now estimated as having a gross size of over $1 trillion, although its own economy has generally weakened relative to other OECD countries. Even with the previous tight exchange control, which acted as a membrane between the Euro-currency market and internal U.K. markets to prevent any ill effects on domestic money policy, a free Euro-currency market existed in London. Great Britain, in fact, has limited sterling capital to lend to the rest of the world, but possesses a great array of commercial and merchant banks, and insurance and shipping companies, together forming the "City of London", which produces several billion dollars in invisible earnings annually.

In banking, this kind of structure is designated a *"turn-table"* market—taking other countries' funds and lending them on again while profiting from the resultant spreads and management fees. Hong Kong and Singapore have successfully copied Britain in creating similar dollar markets, further encouraged in both cases by low taxes on banking income. In the absence of competition in this area from Japan, both centres have grown rather rapidly and constitute an Asian dollar market of nearly $65 billion in Singapore and over $10 billion in Hong Kong. After only a few years, they already offer considerable flexibility and usefulness for Asian lenders and borrowers.

But these cities are not the natural financial leaders of Asia. Hong Kong has only a handful of international banks and MNCs, Singapore hardly any. They have jumped successfully into this area because, to date, the Japanese government has not been willing to let an external dollar market evolve in Tokyo and their own governments have seen the concrete advantages of creating such a mechanism.

Traditional System of Exchange Control

Until recently, there were official barriers to an offshore dollar centre based in Tokyo. Japan, since the Second World War, maintained a tough, "negative" exchange control, like that of Great Britain in the same period. Under a negative system, external transactions are prohibited unless specifically authorised by the central bank or its agents in the form of foreign exchange banks. The Japanese studied European models in creating exchange control laws; the system in use from the late 1940s was approximately that used by the U.K.

Capital transactions with the rest of the world were specifically controlled and no loan could be made into or out of Japan without specific permission. Investment into Japan or abroad, whether portfolio or direct, was similarly restricted. Trade transactions were given precise limits as to final maturity and credit method and foreign exchange exposure management techniques had to follow these limits.

There is nothing unusual in such a structure, particularly in a country which for many years was rebuilding after a major war. (Of course, the Germans have also shown that a similarly dynamic country recovering from an equally disastrous devastation could achieve rapid growth without official controls.)

Related to this framework and the rigorous direction of the economy from above was the prohibition of foreign direct investment into Japan in most industries until the early 1970s and refusal to let foreign banks into this country in any meaningful way until 1969.

Move to Positive Exchange Control

Owing to gradual recognition that strict exchange controls were inconsistent with Japanese economic development, the authorities have undertaken several stages of relaxation. The first, in 1977, liberalised trade transactions, allowing longer payments terms for exports and imports and certain retained currency operations. Changes in 1978 liberalised remaining trade areas and most short-term capital transactions between residents and non-residents with the exception of lending. Thus, Japanese citizens, after 1978, could for the first time invest freely in foreign securities, open banking accounts in foreign currencies at home and abroad or draw unlimited funds for foreign travel. Foreigners could invest freely in the Japanese stock markets or maintain domestic yen accounts without restriction.

In 1980, the Diet voted to move to a "positive" exchange control system, in which all money flows, such as capital transactions and settlement terms for trade transactions and invisible trade would be allowed unless specifically prohibited. For example, impact loans are fully free, only advance notice being necessary. Security transactions are likewise liberalised, security investments and bond issues unrestricted except for advance notice. Direct investment into Japan has become free in principal except for specialised industries, such as defence, agriculture and banking.

In this scheme, the parties drafting the bill allowed very significant loopholes: if (a) the foreign exchange market is chaotic, or (b) the Balance of Payments is deteriorating, or (c) "financial confusion" occurs, liberalisation can be overridden and any transactions brought back within government control.

One or more of the three types of loop-hole conditions have existed at any time in the last decade. In 1980, Japan has seen a chaotic exchange market, a deteriorating Balance of Payments and financial confusion all together. Assuming that the Japanese authorities really meant to liberalise foreign exchange control, a more fundamental question can be raised: who, externally, was calling for such changes? There are still massive problems dividing the Japanese and their trading partners, particularly in the area of bilateral trade imbalances. The U.S.-Japan trade imbalance, for example, remains enormous and unacceptable. The surplus in favour of Japan in 1979 was $9 billion (after $12 billion in 1978) in a time of economic weakness in the U.S., but there is much latent animosity—particularly in the auto section—which can flare up as Japanese exports resume their well-known strength.

Exchange control is not one of the invisible barriers to trade in Japan, but rather more of an annoyance and a cost factor for companies trading in this country; it was not much different from other exchange control frameworks in Europe. What should be scrapped are artificialities in the money markets and the tax and regulatory restrictions inhibiting the growth of a dollar or Euro-currency market in Tokyo.

Factors Inhibiting an Off-shore Market

Three factors have inhibited a Euro-dollar type market from developing in Japan: withholding tax on interest paid to non-residents, the minimum reserve requirements imposed on borrowings from abroad, and the direction of the financial authorities as to the volume, apportionment, rate and other features of external loans. All three of these controls would have to be abolished for a Euro-dollar market to be viable. The first two do not have any serious rationale; little if any tax revenues are created if the underlying transactions are thereby curtailed. The reserve requirement is imposed at the rate of 1/4%. However, the maximum rate is 3%; this could go up at any time and fear of this eventuality inhibits many transactions. Since reserve requirements are not used as an instrument of monetary policy in Japan, it seems unnecessary to require them in a field of endeavour, which has been little seen in Japan except for impact loan funding.

As argued in Chapter Four, allocation of financial resources is unlikely to be efficiently made by government setting of volumes and interest rates. (There is, of course, a different argument for banking prudence and the theme of this chapter does not speak against ratios being set for banks' foreign currency asset and liability matching, nor overall limits of capital to assets or capital to individual country risks.) More efficiency is likely obtained when financial institutions compete freely on the basis of their comparative advantages; in this specific case, they should be allowed that freedom in a Tokyo off-shore dollar market, which participants in other off-shore markets already enjoy.

Such a dollar market has traditionally been opposed by the authorities. As stated throughout this text, many bureaucrats wish thereby to protect the domestic economy, which they see as fragile. Younger officials are more appreciative of the benefits of a dollar market, but usually indicate that development of the yen market must come first.

Need for Invisible Income

There is no contradiction in the liberalisation of both yen and dollar markets in the same period. Japan now is showing large deficits in its current account and had one of the largest current account deficits of any country in 1980. While much of this is due to oil and other commodity price increases, part is also due to Japan's deficit in invisible account. Development of a *"City of*

Tokyo" would develop several billion dollars of annual invisible income in the future, as does the City of London. The resultant improvement of the current account would be all the more striking and necessary if one accepts the probability that Japanese export surpluses of the past magnitude may no longer be tolerated. Japan is likely to have less ability to generate huge external surpluses because of the increasing cost of its energy and raw materials. It may be adversely affected by high labour costs and by the attempts by its trading rivals to stop such export surpluses from appearing again. Measures in that regard, if worse comes to worst, would certainly include much sharper import quotas and tariff walls.

Increases in invisible income create little friction. Few people, if any, are put out of work by more competition in the banking sector, although many new jobs would be created in Tokyo. Japan, with its multinational banks and multinational companies, is the natural centre of finance in the Far East. Its economy is the great engine of Asia. There is little hope for the present centres of Hong Kong and Singapore to withstand Japan's financial prowess, except by reason of their tax concessions, if the changes listed above are made and a competing dollar market is allowed to develop in Tokyo.

Thus, the Japanese authorities may be overlooking an area of significant future potential by stressing exchange control and other piece-meal liberalisation rather than off-shore dollar market development. A *"City of Tokyo"* is a natural and increasingly necessary evolution. Exchange control liberalisation has a pleasant modernising ring, but is not an area of national necessity. Indeed, an argument can be made that many capital transactions should remain under some direct control if they enter or leave Japan's economy. A dynamic, aggressive and arbitrage-seeking Asian-dollar market based in Tokyo *might* affect the monetary or fiscal policy of Japan if the world continues to be as chaotic as it has been recently. If no one is insisting upon exchange control liberalisation, then perhaps that mechanism's ability to limit the effect of external markets on the internal economy should have been maintained.

The present over-emphasis on exports would diminish if a sophisticated international market develops in Japan. All major economic sectors of Japan would benefit, including the government, which would get more taxes from the increased revenues of locally based banks. Banking in this form—and invisible income in general—is not controversial and does not create the types of acrimonious dialogue Japan now has with the rest of the world. The world's financial markets have three natural centres: New York, London and Tokyo. Little has to be done for Japan to take its place in that constellation.

II

USING THE SYSTEM

A. Sources of Credit

CHAPTER 7

Sources of Credit/Relationship Factors

This chapter summarises the types of domestic credit facilities available in Japan, alternative sources of finance and the relationship factors which plan an important and idiosyncratic role in that country.

BANK SOURCES

Short-term Facilities: Yen

Short-term *working capital facilities* are available from city, regional, local and foreign banks. Depending on the credit of the borrower, loans are extended in the form of clean advances, usually for 90 days, or discounts of trade bill receivables. A more limited class of trade bill—from manufacturer to first wholesaler only—can be rediscounted by commercial banks at the Bank of Japan; such credits may have particularly advantageous interest rates.

Lines of credit, as commonly used and understood abroad, are not a usual type of facility in Japan; more typically, a borrower will discuss forthcoming credit needs for a three- or six-month period, current financial data and collateral offered with his house banks in advance. They will agree on terms and conditions and both the borrower and lender will feel committed to take down and extend the credit, respectively. Credit facilities tend to be used continuously, thus discussion revolves around changes in rates and other services used.

Overdrafts are considerably less prevalent than in Western European markets. Although this credit form exists, it is not favoured by Japanese banks, which prefer regular and longer maturity borrowings. Less than 1% of Japanese bank loan balances are in the form of overdrafts at any usual month-end, although they may be larger during the month. The problem of credit ceilings is at times very severe for the Japanese city banks, already overlent and supporting giant corporations which are overborrowed in Western terms. The unpredictability of overdrafts makes limit control harder; unexpected drawdowns can push a bank over its credit ceiling at quarter end.

Stamp tax applies in Japan on promissory notes and bills of exchange, but not on overdrafts or clean advances. The stamp tax is graduated, rising to ¥50,000 on bills of over ¥500 million. This cost is borne by the borrower, whose natural tendency is to lengthen borrowings to three or six months to minimise the tax in effective per annum percentage terms. Extending the tenor can give a rate advantage to the borrower in times of increasing interest rates and may be opposed.

Nominal interest rates on short-term credits extended by Japanese banks are invariably tied to the official discount rate of the Bank of Japan. The "prime rate" for short-term facilities offered by Japanese banks has for many years been nominally $\frac{1}{4}$% over the official discount rate.[1] This is misleading, as *compensating balances* push up the actual cost of funds appreciably. It is forbidden to tie specifically compensating balances to a loan, but they are expected and required for every borrower, causing effective rates to be higher than nominal ones. This practice brings many advantages to the banks: higher than average gross borrowings, added liquidity, increased income. Problems for borrowers when credit ceilings are in force arise, because they may need to borrow 20–30% or even more than actually required to cover net needs, and their banks may be under pressure to hold down outstanding credits. A further advantage to the Japanese banks of compensating balances is avoiding the usury ceiling. Under the "Temporary Interest Rate Law" of 1947—still fully in effect, short-term rates for advances cannot exceed 2% over the discount rate, nor overdraft rates more than 3%. At the time of writing, the official discount rate stood at 7.25% and the short-term "prime" rate at 7.5%, but the average effective borrowing cost for large corporations was around 8.8% and some small companies were effectively paying 9.5% or more. At times of a severe credit squeeze, the pressure on corporations to put up higher and higher compensating balances intensifies; balances of 50% are not unheard of.

Short-term and other facilities are governed not only by collateral, cash flows and offsettable compensating balances, but also by banks' **General Business Conditions**. These conditions, accepted by a borrowing client upon establishment of a relationship, give Japanese banks rights to take assets, seize collateral or offset holdings to counter possible losses in event of threatened insolvency even though there is no literal default. The concatenation of negative and positive pledges found in the average Western (particularly U.S.) loan agreement is *not* spelled out; there may be no credit agreement at all. But the General Business Conditions, which are the same for all banks, give greater powers than do most formal agreements.

Not only are balances and collateral protection weighted in favour of the lender, but also the transactional side of payment and exchange business traditionally compensates the bank for its assistance as well. Customers are expected to allocate foreign exchange conversions, payments and letters of credit to their banks in a ratio closely related to the percentage of credit each extends.

Foreign Currency

Both bankers' acceptances in dollars and relatively short-term impact loans in a variety of currencies are available.

Dollar Bankers' Acceptances are used for import financing by large trading houses, commodity and general importers, particularly by crude oil buyers. The bank accepting the draft will likely rediscount it directly in the New York Bankers' Acceptance market, the rates in which set the basis for costs of dollar acceptance financing in Japan.

Short-term impact loans are credits in foreign currency, formerly made for a specific project, but now available for general purposes. These loans can be negotiated in various convertible currencies, including some of the Middle Eastern ones, in both fixed and floating rates. Rates and spreads closely follow market rates in London or other Euro-centres. Impact loan permission, necessary until 1980 for each transaction, was rarely given to foreign-controlled companies. After the liberalisation of exchange control in that year, only prior notice of foreign currency borrowing is necessary; rate, term and conditions are in theory free.

Long-term Credit: Yen

The chief sources of long-term credit are the trust and long-term banks, as well as specialised government banks such as Japan Development Bank. Long-term loans are predominantly used for expansion of physical facilities: plant, equipment, land or permanent inventory. This area has been in many ways more important historically than at the beginning of the 1980s, when the great capital investment programme of Japan can be seen to have matured.

Collateral

Invariably, long-term loans are made with security of the underlying assets to be financed. This is typically done with a mortgage or direct pledge of assets.

Rate

The majority of long-term loans are based on the long-term "prime rate"—a rate set from time to time by the long-term banks association under influence from the Bank of Japan. Few loans to domestic borrowers, however, maintain the same effective rate over their life. Compensating balances may be required in long-term loans as well, to increase the effective yield of a fixed rate loan.

Foreign Currency
Impact loans

These facilities range to seven years, although maturities of five years are more widely found. Either bullet or amortised loans can be negotiated; many currencies are available. Japanese banks may make such loans since 1980, breaking the monopoly of foreign bank branches. Interest rates follow those of the Eurocurrency involved. Five-year dollar impact loans in late 1980, for instance, could be obtained by prime Japanese borrowers for $3/8\%$ over LIBO throughout, or for $1/2\%$ by average borrowers. This compares favourably to sovereign risk interest rates paid by most OECD countries.

NON-BANK SOURCES

Intercompany loans from abroad

Parent company loans to their Japanese subsidiaries are a common source of non-bank finance. Such loans must be reported before completion and at least a one-month "no-action" period ensues before the loan can be made, if it is to be for more than one year. Terms should not vary widely from arms' length market rates. Loans can be in parent currency or in yen, although the source of yen in that case should not be *Euro-yen*, but yen developed by the parent from domestic sources or bought spot. The waiting period before making inward loans will depend in part on the current status of the Japanese Balance of Payments, i.e. whether the authorities are discouraging or encouraging foreign capital inflows.

Parallel loans

In certain cases, parallel loan transactions can develop local yen credit in return for home country currency being extended to a subsidiary of the Japanese lender. Two domestic transactions are involved and Ministry of Finance approval is not required. In a typical transaction, the Japanese subsidiary of a multinational firm receives a term yen credit from a Japanese company; a foreign subsidiary of that Japanese firm receives credit in equal amount and term from the foreign parent. Rates are related to the equivalent long-term market in both countries. Since disintermediation is involved, the partners in the transaction all benefit: financing is cheaper than equivalent bank sources and funds invested at better than bank deposit or bond market rates. The bank putting the transactions together will receive a fee and may guarantee one or both sides of the credit.

Gensaki borrowings

Gensaki in Japanese refers to a spot/forward transaction involving a sale and purchase back of securities, akin to a "repo" in U.S. practice. *Gensaki* deals arose as the result of attempts to circumvent interest ceilings on deposits; corporations could buy and resell securities in closed transactions through securities houses with their excess cash and earn thereby money market, as opposed to administered bank deposit, rates. Corporations needing cash can borrow in a converse way, selling securities in portfolio and repurchasing them later. *Gensaki* rates are more closely related to true costs of funds; yet it is imprudent to rely on such deals permanently, as they are unpredictable and not welcomed by the Bank of Japan.

Long-dated swaps

The Japanese foreign exchange market remains an imperfect one (see Chapter Twelve) and it is possible at times to borrow a foreign currency, sell it spot against yen and simultaneously buy it forward, creating thereby long-term yen often at a net cost below that of normal long-term loans. This type of credit, however, is sporadic and usually available only from imaginative foreign bank branches. While attractive if all the variables coalesce, it is a question of luck whether a long-dated swap (the sale of yen against the currency several years forward) can be attained.

Leasing

Japanese leasing companies have reached large size and technical ability; Orient Leasing Company (a Sanwa Bank affiliate) is the world's largest leasing entity in terms of assets leased. Leasing of buildings, computers, office equipment, vehicle fleets, etc., has grown significantly and can be compared to Western leasing availability. Tax and balance sheet considerations of leasing are similar to those elsewhere.

Factoring

Factoring has also been developed, following Western examples. A number of factoring companies have been created in Japan; they, like their foreign counterparts, take over receivables from manufacturing or trading entities at a discount cost based on market rates. In these transactions, compensating balances do not apply, credit can be obtained even if house banks have reached their ceilings, and non-recourse finance may be negotiated.

BANK RELATIONSHIP FACTORS

Historical Relevance

As noted above, bank finance was essential to the development of Japan in its fastest growth periods of Meiji and post-World War II. In both periods, evergreen credit from commercial banks substituted for equity capital financing and became the primary source of funds for Japanese industrial growth. Banks were in effect partners of corporations, acting more like subordinated debt holders than short-term suppliers of funds. Success of their over-borrowed customers was critical to over-lent banks, which often had ownership shares in, as well as loans to, enterprise. In addition to being a financial partner, the banks also acted as treasurer and financial adviser to the same companies. In the most striking cases, company/bank integration developed to the *Zaibatsu* stage, business combinations of extraordinary power and cohesion. Even in non-*Zaibatsu* relationships, the combination/partnership/mutual assistance of banks and companies goes beyond the bounds of other companies.

The combination of state guidance and company and bank mutual support coalesces in the often-discussed *Japan Inc.*, a term used to connote the joint decision-making and mutuality of interests of these groups. It is true that Japan's modernisation and export drive are discussed between, and fostered by tacit co-operation of, all three sectors. Also understood is that a major component—company or bank—of *Japan Inc.* will not be allowed to fail. For instance, Japanese government officials indicate emphatically, if privately, that none of the top banks in Japan will be allowed to fail (i.e. the city, trust, long-term and regional banks) although mergers are possible. A leading member of a Japanese "core" industry: heavy machinery, shipbuilding, chemical, electronics, auto, trading, will likewise likely be saved from bankruptcy by state intervention. This was shown graphically in the Ataka case.

Ataka was the fourth largest Japanese trading company in the early 1970s. It extended trade credit in excessive amounts to a Newfoundland refinery for crude oil purchases. The unpaid receivables broke the company. Its viable assets were eventually merged into C. Itoh, another large trading house, but the resultant loss of some $370 million from dead receivables and bankrupt business sectors was absorbed by its house banks: Sumitomo Bank and Kyowa Bank. Foreign creditors, although basically unsecured, lost nothing. (Sumitomo was able to write off its massive loss largely against hidden reserves and tax credits.)

Foreign banks in and outside of Japan spend considerable time deciphering which companies are part or not part of *Japan Inc.* as an aid to credit decisions. While the concept has some validity, it is unwise to use it as the basis of credit extension. So far, only Japanese banks have borne the brunt of any losses from bankruptcy or reorganisation of companies in trouble.[2] But certain foreign bank branches are reaching high figures in their aggregate lending to single Japanese companies; it is probable that they will have to step up for their share of losses if such a creditor fails. Far better to posit lending to Japanese corporations on the basis of full analysis of financial statements and trends, cash flow projections and collateral. However, one can safely state that major Japanese banks will not be allowed to fail, nor default on any *external* obligations, to protect Japan's financial reputation abroad.

Adding to the close relationship of companies and banks over many decades in Japanese financial history are the scars left from the oil crisis of 1973/74. After the three-fold rise in the price of crude oil, the Japanese Balance of Payments deteriorated sharply and moved into overall deficit. The Consumer Price Index rose sharply; to combat both problems a draconian monetary policy was enforced. Sharp limits on yen credit ensued; interest rates soared. Even large companies could not get enough credit for their working capital requirements with inflation sharply rising and extreme credit strictness rule. (Foreign currency borrowing as a result boomed; during that period foreign bank branches in Tokyo finally were able to increase assets at high spreads at a rapid pace.) This experience of total unavailability of new domestic credit was a searing one and many finance managers still base bank relationships on making sure that sufficient credit will be available during the next squeeze.

Effects of Bank Relationships

Both companies and bank profit from their unusually close relationship. The borrower, by giving his house banks generous compensating deposits and foreign exchange and other business and maintaining loan balances even when not needed, is assured of continued credit and support. The banks can count on relatively constant footings—even if the macro-economy and its micro-sectors are liquid—and from excess balances, higher effective rates of return. A Western company, however, may not see this relationship in the same way. Treasurers of multinational subsidiaries in Japan have head offices which harp on the fact that there are apparently excess amounts of cash sitting around. Much time is spent explaining that these deposits are compensating ones, insisted upon by the banks to bring effective yields higher. Since it is difficult to maintain exactly the right level of balances, excess balances (higher yields to the lenders) are typical. The moral support and implied permanent support of the Japanese lenders may be unapparent or unimportant to the foreign company, which will likely weigh its bank needs more coldly. Japanese borrowing will in almost every case be a small percentage of world-wide needs and Japanese banks will rarely be seen as house banks.

How to Use Relationship Factors

How, then, should the foreign subsidiary approach this idiosyncratic system of relationships and compensating balances? If it succumbs to the Japanese mystique that house banks are protectors of industry, that financial matters can be entrusted to their hands and that borrowings of any nature are effectively permanent, cash management in Western style will be interrupted. Excess balances, from a mathematical point of view, will be maintained. Foreign exchange will be allocated by relationship, not rate, as will be other banking services. (It is probable that the Japanese staff of a Western subsidiary or joint venture will promote this approach to their banking needs; Chapter Thirteen gives a portrayal of the personnel conflicts thereby arising.)

To push cash management too far and thereby neglect Japanese concepts of bank relationships is risky. There may be a repeat of the credit crunch of 1974 (the early 1980s are a likely period for such a recurrence) and foreign subsidiaries will be among the most affected. Good relationships with and tapping of the increasingly strong abilities of Japanese banks can be profitable. What is needed is to transmute a local Japanese bank relationship into a world one, in which what the multinational company has to offer to the Japanese side is pointed out in global terms. The foreign subsidiary likely needs constant help, but at reasonable effective costs in Japan. Its strict observance of effective rates and relatively small borrowing needs in most cases are of only marginal interest to the Japanese lender. Using the lure of business from parent and other subsidiaries may help a foreign subsidiary to negotiate better terms in Japan and avoid the negative and costly aspects of the relationship factors faced by Japanese firms.

(1) In early 1981, the short-term prime unusually stood at $\frac{1}{2}$% over the official discount rate.
(2) Several foreign banks in Japan faced massive losses in mid-1981 after having lent to small companies which went bankrupt after a major stock speculation scandal.

CHAPTER 8

Role of the Foreign Banks

Tucked away in the financial statistics of Japan—almost lost in the rounding off—is the lending business of a group of some 70 foreign banks. These institutions made up 3.4% of all Japanese bank loans at the end of 1979; if foreign currency denominated loan assets are eliminated, the foreign banks in Japan extend less than 1% of the yen crédits made by resident institutions. This is a very small position when compared to foreign banks in the U.S., U.K. or Germany; and many of the foreign participants are likely to be in the red on a fully costed basis. The following treats the background of foreign bank penetration in Japan, their present activities, the services they can offer to corporate treasurers and the outlook for their future growth.

Background to Foreign Bank Entry

The reasons for foreign banks establishing operating units in Japan are much the same as those which took British, U.S. and later Continental European banks, to other centres: an attractive, large market with massive local capital requirements, investment by multinationals of their home country and close relations with Japanese correspondents. Some banks saw this very early; a Citibank predecessor established a Tokyo branch in 1913, a courageous step and one which has paid off handsomely over the years. Between the World Wars, few foreign banks tried to establish such branches, but'many helped in the modernisation of Japanese industry and rebuilding after the Great Kanto Earthquake of 1923. J.P. Morgan and Co., for example, became the chief investment house for the Japanese Government in that period, underwriting the Reconstruction Bonds of 1923 and the City of Tokyo issue of 1924. Guaranty Trust Company underwrote the Tokyo Electric Power and the Tohoku Electric bond issues shortly thereafter.

World War II severed foreign banking ties; after 1945 a handful of banks re-established their branches or started new ones during the occupation. Thereafter, however, direct inward investment in banking was not allowed for many years, just as most industry areas were also precluded from having wholly-owned subsidiaries. A few indirect entries were seen before 1969;

Continental Illinois was able to buy a Dutch bank long resident in Japan in the 1950s, but most of the world's largest banks were excluded, despite the advent of many Japanese branches or "agencies" tantamount to branches abroad in the 1960s. In 1969, Morgan Guaranty was allowed to open a Tokyo branch, which signalled a shift in policy. Now banks from most major countries, except Saudi Arabia and Australia (and Texas) where reciprocity is still an issue, are represented. Table 8.1 shows the foreign banks in Japan as of 31 March 1979.

Monopoly of "Impact" Loans in the Past

A major business strategy for new foreign branches, which were generally not permitted to solicit deposits or advertise, was to concentrate on extending foreign currency "impact" loans. These loans were authorised in the early 1950s, when Japanese companies, needing more capital to rebuild than could be developed at home, negotiated term credits from foreign banks, usually in dollars. The "impact" was seen in reconstruction; loans were individually approved and had to be used for specific plant and equipment investment. As foreign banks opened branches in Tokyo, off-shore impact loan balances were transferred to the new entities, giving them an immediate asset base. Any MOF or BOJ dollar deposits were also transferred to the branches as well. New impact loans were booked in Tokyo thereafter to build up the local operation and to avoid tax complications. (Even if an impact loan is made from New York or elsewhere, its income will be ascribed to the Japanese branch if there is involvement from Tokyo. With problems of distance and communications, it is difficult to imagine impact loans not going through a Tokyo branch if one exists.)

Impact loan monopoly was given to the foreign banks for two reasons. This relatively small niche would serve to give enough income to keep foreign banks above water; individual control by BOJ over each loan—including rate and terms—could ensure proper allocation of foreign currency loan volume and distribution. Competition with Japanese banks and effects, if any, on yen lending volumes and practices would be diminished. More cynical was the knowledge that if something disastrous happened in the Euro-dollar markets, making dollar funding difficult or mismatching of borrowings unprofitable, the head offices of foreign banks would have to bail them out. If Japanese banks were so caught, it would be the Bank of Japan which ultimately would launch the rescue.

Owing to this background, impact loan business has developed over the years and become the mainstay of foreign bank activity. Because of the paucity of yen funds available to foreign branches, their balance sheets have built up around a base of impact loans. After the oil shock of 1973/74, when a Draconian credit squeeze was imposed on yen availability, the foreign banks had an unparalleled opportunity to make currency loans (and to refinance bankers' acceptances) at very good spreads. In 1974/75 loans with average maturities

Table 8.1
Foreign Banks in Japan (as of the end of March 1979)

Nationality	Number of Banks	Number of Branches	Number of Representative Offices
U.S.A.	36	33	14
Canada	5	—	5
Europe	65	32	46
U.K.	19	11	11
France	12	7	8
Germany	7	5	5
Switzerland	6	3	5
Italy	5	1	4
Netherlands	3	4	1
Belgium	3	1	2
Luxembourg	2	—	2
Denmark	2	—	2
Spain	2	—	2
Sweden	2	—	2
Finland	1	—	1
Norway	1	—	1
Oceania	8	—	8
Australia	7	—	7
New Zealand	1	—	1
Central & South America	7	2	5
Mexico	3	—	3
Brazil	2	2	—
Peru	1	—	1
Cuba	1	—	1
Asia	23	17	11
Korea	9	4	7
Singapore	4	4	—
India	2	2	1
Indonesia	2	1	1
Malaysia	1	1	—
Philippines	1	—	1
Rep. of China	1	2	—
Thailand	1	2	—
Pakistan	1	1	—
Iran	1	—	1
Total	144	84	89

Source: Federation of Bankers Association of Japan

70

of five years were booked at effective rates of $1\frac{1}{2}\%$ or more over LIBO. The development of foreign bank business jumped far above a long-term trend line, both in the aggregate and for most individual banks, as indicated in Table 8.2.

Size and Profitability of the Foreign Banks

The foreign bank branches in Japan can be divided into three classes. The "Big Three": Citibank, Bank of America and Chase had about $3 billion each in footings on 31 March 1980 and account for some 40% of all foreign bank assets. The next group comprises a number of world-class banks whose Tokyo branches range between $1–2 billion: Morgan, Deutsche, Manufacturers Hanover. The third and largest class includes all the newcomers who followed the others to Tokyo in the early and mid-1970s. Many of these are still small and are struggling for a role to play.

The size and profitability of an individual foreign branch in Tokyo will depend in large part on when it came, as well as what it can offer elsewhere to Japanese banks and corporations. If a branch began operations early enough to capitalise on the oil crisis, it probably was able to build up an asset base of impact loans and some yen loans and enter a position of self-sustained growth. If it came later, loans of any kind became harder to develop and spreads were

Table 8.2

Growth of Foreign Bank Branches' Assets in Japan, 1971/78

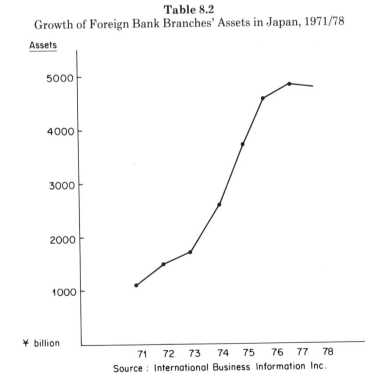

Source : International Business Information Inc.

much smaller. As a general rule, returns on assets peaked, as could be expected, in 1974/75 and have been declining since.

Impact loans will likely play a smaller role in Japan in the future; Japanese banks have been able to make any kind of impact loan since 1 January 1980, which bodes poorly for foreign banks. Depending on a dollar framework is in any case artificial for banks seeking to operate in the long run in Japan. Foreign banking institutions must become yen-based (which presents them with the challenge of obtaining yen funding), play a role in recycling balance of payments flows and extend their expertise and special services to Japanese companies.

Yen funding remains the quintessential problem. Foreign banks have the right to create yen from dollar swaps, within limits which have been increased from time to time, but they are in general quite restricted in their ability to raise yen funds. Their yen sources are: capital and reserves, customer deposits, yen created through swaps, bill discounting, call money borrowing and lines from correspondent banks. Access to all these sources is limited by government policy or by structural factors.

Because there are minimal capital requirements and no limitations have so far been set on their loans as a ratio of capital, none of the branches have large capital accounts. Similarly, as foreign banks were not permitted (until 1979) to solicit deposits actively and most have only one wholesale branch, they attract very few deposits, except those directly from borrowing customers. Not only is their ability to create yen through swaps restricted, but also swap limits are denominated in dollars and yen funding thus is unpredictable. Many foreign branches have urged the authorities to consider sharply increasing their swap limits in line with the yen's appreciation, although most recognise that it would be difficult to remove limits on swaps entirely. Swap quotas would ideally be denominated in yen; this would allow more structured and better planned liability management. More marginal funding is obtained when branches sell their bills (promissory notes collateralised by yen loans to major companies), borrow call money, take deposits from correspondent banks or issue a limited amount of CDs.

Table 8.3
Return on Assets Trends: Foreign Banks in Japan, 1972/79

	1972	1973	1974	1975	1976	1977	1978	1979
Earnings (¥ billion)	15.7	18.1	29.9	40.6	41.5	34.2	29.7	17.8
Return on assets (%)	n.a.	1.03	1.19	1.12	.93	.70	.60	.29
Asset growth rate (%)	35	13.3	57.4	27.9	21.6	8.3	−2.7	54.9*

* Misleading, owing to sharp depreciation of the yen and corresponding appreciation of dollar assets. Likewise, 1978 is understated for converse reasons.
Source: International Business Information Incorporated

Not only are lending opportunities limited by Japanese company/bank relationships, but funding costs are also generally higher than Japanese banks. Foreign banks depend largely on borrowed or swapped funds, which cost far more than local yen deposits, for which artificially low interest rates may be set. On average, foreign banks' interest rates can be estimated to be about 1% above those of competing Japanese banks for prime credits. Chiefly at times of a *waku* on Japanese competitors does yen loan demand act counter to a long-range decline. Only when the forward premium on the yen is larger than the interest parity factor can foreign banks compete on a price basis; otherwise, they must depend on relationship factors and special services to convince local customers to borrow yen from this source.

What Foreign Banks Offer

What, then, do foreign banks offer in Japan in the 1980s? Seen in national terms, they are a useful goad to the Japanese banks. The Japanese authorities see foreign institutions as bringing ideas to Japan which may widen the range of banking and increase competition at home. Foreign banks import techniques such as consumer finance in Japan and encourage cash management tools such as overdrafts; Japanese industry benefits and Japanese banks develop. The irritation of dealing with blue-eyed, moustached foreigners is a small price to pay if Japan's financial structure is helped (a reason also why representatives of merchant banks are tolerated in Tokyo, despite the grey area they inhabit between commercial banks and securities houses).

This educational role, however, is clearly a transitory one. The Japanese banks are ever more aggressive at home and abroad and may be slowly moving towards universal bank status. A real question for the foreign banks in Japan is what their role will be in the Japan of the future, when the Japanese have full world-wide networks, greater expertise and full services at home.

Presently, the foreign branches can compete by stressing six general areas:
— a wider range of yen facilities;
— multi-currency option impact loans and loans in a variety of "exotic" currencies;
— foreign exchange expertise;
— international financial expertise, including special transactions such as parallel loans, four-party swaps, and very long-dated forwards;
— merchant banking; and
— overseas services.

Different Yen Facilities

Because of their higher cost structure, foreign banks have to offer a wider range and more flexible package of yen facilities. Because the foreign banks and their major multinational customers are accustomed to overdraft facilities in other markets, they were the first aggressively to offer overdrafts in Japan. These facilities account for up to 10% of the lines of certain foreign banks in Tokyo and usage is thought to be active. In the recent borrowers' market, there has been no cost differential between overdrafts and 90-day advances. Corporate treasurers have been able to use these facilities flexibly, reducing thereby net outstanding borrowings. Overdrafts have particularly been utilised by foreign companies, which are generally more concerned with maximising cash management benefits. In the longer term area, certain foreign banks also fill a gap between the relatively short-term lending of the city banks and the longer-term lending of the trust and long-term banks. It can be difficult, for example, to obtain three-, four- or five-year fixed-rate yen loans, as this tenor falls between the funding sources of the two major groups of Japanese domestic banks. Foreign banks, starting in 1978, were aggressive in providing fixed-rate medium-term yen loans at prices significantly below the long-term prime and with no compensating balances. They were able to do so by taking one of three strategies:

1) Running an unmatched position, i.e., lending long and funding short in the hope that rate movements would, over time, allow an adequate spread.

2) Finding long-term sources of funds from some of the large agricultural co-operative banks which have been flush with funds but which have a small corporate customer base. These institutions were pleased to lend funds at competitive fixed rates to foreign banks which could re-lend them, making up in some part for their total lack of long-term deposits. The co-operative institutions received foreign currency deposits or facilities from the head offices of foreign banks, helpful allies in the co-operatives' planned expansion into the international market.

3) By long-term swaps. For example, a foreign bank can borrow dollars up to five years, buy spot yen and cover by selling the yen forward for the same period. Given the imperfection of the Japanese market, the net cost of medium-term yen created in this way can be below the long-term prime; the foreign banks could lend competitively. Constraints here are the limited nature of the market for forward dollar/yen after about two years, and also that the yen thereby created fall under swap limits, which are primarily used to create funding for short-term facilities.

Multi-currency Loans

Foreign banks include a variety of currencies in their impact loan lending and are likely to be more competitive in this area than the Japanese banks. For example, they have made large loans in Kuwaiti dinars, Saudi riyals and Bahraini dinars, all of which are of interest to Japanese borrowers with contracts in the Middle East. Loans in all the major Euro-currencies have been negotiated on a floating or fixed-rate basis. Impact loans now routinely have multi-currency option clauses, so that the borrower can pick which currency to borrow at each rollover date.

Foreign Exchange Expertise

The foreign exchange capabilities of the largest U.S. and European banks are equal to or above those of their Japanese competitors, with the exception of the Bank of Tokyo. Although Tokyo branches of foreign banks are quite limited in their net open positions against yen, they are able to provide a broader range of foreign exchange expertise and advice in Tokyo than otherwise available. Several have established foreign exchange advisory teams which work directly with corporate customers, advising them as to market developments and hedging strategies. Some foreign banks also make a true market in the long-dated forwards mentioned above; they are willing to quote realistic rates up to five years and take these into their position or lay them off abroad. Such quotes are not readily available from other sources.

International Financial Expertise

Foreign banks have the ability to draw upon their multinational network to come up with a wide range of sophisticated services, which can be utilised by corporate treasurers in Japan. A typical example of this are the four-party parallel loans which recently have been put together in the Tokyo market.

Merchant Banking

Many European universal banks and U.S. commercial banks have begun merchant banking activities in Tokyo through representative offices. These offices are able to help resident companies in Japan with both funding and investment strategies. Private placements in foreign currencies, as well as direct public issues, are arranged by the head offices or merchant bank arms of such institutions and floating rate note or CD issues of Japanese banks abroad underwritten. Conversely, excess funds of Japanese foreign subsidiaries can be utilised in a number of ways. Such merchant banks' representatives are often active in the type of special multi-currency deals described above.

Overseas Services

Using their overseas networks, foreign banks can provide excellent cash management and international money management (IMM) services. They are able to accelerate export collections, manage and optimise the use of cash held abroad and assist the use of intermediary vehicles. Obviously, they can make market surveys for potential investors and offer the necessary investment and working capital finance thereafter.

Future Growth of Foreign Banks in Japan

Their special expertise in international financial transactions has allowed some foreign banks a relatively attractive role to play in a period where impact loans have been diminishing in overall volume and spread. Future growth will depend upon two important factors: the ability to develop yen funding and the growth of Tokyo into a world financial market. Both these await liberalisation of Japanese financial regulations.

It is important for foreign banks to increase their yen base, as the secular decline of impact loans will make that asset too small a foundation on which to build their increasingly expensive operations. Competition of Japanese banks in dollar impact loans, if not in other currencies, will hasten this decline. Foreign banks cannot be successful with Japanese multinationals abroad, or as helpful as they wish to be with multinational subsidiaries in Japan, unless they have a wider and more flexible funding base in Japan itself. This will also help retail-oriented banks in their move into consumer finance in Japan. But the foreign branches are dependent on guidelines of BOJ and MOF in a still manipulated marketplace as to the volume of their funding; interest costs are not under their control and cannot be planned.

What foreign banks need is the ability to use more types of instruments along the lines of the recently introduced Certificates of Deposits. They would like to have an unlimited CD quota, and more importantly to be able to issue debentures, but it is improbable that foreign banks will issue debentures or samurai bonds until the Japanese city banks are allowed to do so.

Discrimination, however, is no longer a major issue, as it formerly was. For the last several years, the trade war with America and the EEC has been compounded by complaints of discrimination against the foreign banks. There have been problems of prohibited access to funding in the past, but these are now largely over. The foreign banks can compete on an almost equal basis with city banks in the yen money markets and the problem is more one of artificiality of those markets rather than exclusion. Officials are sensitive to the discrimination issue and it is unlikely that the foreign banks will find themselves in such a position again.

The best chance for foreign banks to become more than a nominal force in Japanese finance is the development of a London-type Euro-dollar market in Tokyo, which would be beneficial for Japan as a whole. That change would allow the foreign banks to capitalise on their main comparative advantage: international market acumen. To be prominent in a Tokyo-based Euro-market would not require a large yen base nor many additional local staff. Trading and deposit experts could be seconded to Tokyo to develop the type of telephone/telex-based market that exists in other world centres. The same institutions which have successfully led Singapore's and Hong Kong's Asian dollar market growth could quickly transplant people and knowledge to Japan; their probable market share would then be far greater than their present one, as it is in dollar/yen exchange trading already.

Whether the Japanese authorities want the foreign banking community to play a larger overall role is a moot point. Building up to the percentage of bank assets gained by Japanese banks in the U.S. or U.S. banks in the United

Kingdom might well be unwanted and thus made impossible. But using foreign banks as the leading edge of a dynamic Asian-dollar market in Tokyo, once that decision is taken, would be characteristic of the way Japanese leaders have used Western knowledge since the Meiji period. The competitive lead of the dominant foreign banks would be accepted in return for the educational and market creative input they bring.

In sum, the foreign banks in Japan are in a transition period, many of them at best in a holding pattern. The monopoly of foreign currency loans, in which they acted as a conduit of foreign capital into Japan, has been opened to all lenders. Their yen base is small; it will be difficult under the present restrictions for them to increase yen funding in more than a marginal way. Their best chance for success is in staying a step ahead of local competition in international dealings and in using their home country strength to help Japanese MNC expansion abroad. Under that presumption, the top U.S. and European banks in Japan should have a vibrant role to play in years to come.

CHAPTER 9

Japanese Bank Lending Abroad

The nature of access to the Japanese capital markets, whether through yen borrowing or bond issues, is directly related to Balance of Payments expectations and recycling of surpluses and these markets cannot yet be considered a permanent source of new liquidity to the rest of the world. Both major types of external borrowing—direct yen loans and bond flotations—are covered by this attitude. Chapter Nine gives a macro-economic explanation of the role of Japanese bank lending abroad, as well as a guide to borrowing terms and conditions. Chapter Ten discusses samurai bonds issued by non-residents.

Financial Market Background

The Japanese capital markets have generally been thin, domestically-oriented and characterised by high rates of interest. Until relatively recently, Japan was a poor country; even in its periods of rapid growth, whatever capital was produced through savings/profits was used by voracious local borrowers. The devastation of World War II and the borrowing of domestic corporations thereafter to rebuild—during a period of 20 years when the real growth rate was 10% per annum—confirmed that pattern. High corporate debt to equity ratios were typical and the local capital markets were never effectively open to the rest of the world. Japanese banks were heavy net borrowers in dollar markets to refinance their own trade and industrial lending. In the early 1970s, Japan did become a net creditor, but soon turned around after the oil shock of 1973/74. After adjustment to that structural change, Japan's economy regained steady growth in the late 1970s, albeit at a reduced rate of around 5% per annum. With concentration on exports, aided by an undervalued yen, the Balance of Payments position of Japan moved into the well-known pattern of enormous trade and current account surpluses, culminating in 1978's current account surplus of $16.5 billion.

In that year and early 1979, Japan's financial markets were characterised by high corporate liquidity. Many Japanese companies were working at low capacity utilisation; few, except electric power generating companies, had important new capital expenditure requirements. Thus, interest rates fell abruptly from late-1975 to mid-1978 from a lack of demand for capital and from a conscious effort on the part of the government to stimulate investment by residents and borrowing by non-residents.

The primary concern of Japan's financial authorities in 1978 became pumping back out Balance of Payment surpluses through long-term capital outflows in the form of credit extended to non-residents, as well as direct foreign investment. With the yen soaring from 300/$ eventually to beyond 180/$ in October 1978, and the resultant expansion of the money supply, recycling of surpluses through increased usage of Japanese capital markets by foreigners became a priority matter. Samurai bonds, yen syndicated loans and yen private placements all increased dramatically in 1978 and 1979. Not only did official policy encourage such outflows, but the drop in interest rates, making yen cheaper than dollar loans, complemented the demand for yen borrowings.

Motivation of Japanese Lenders

Liquidity in Japan and slowing of demand from domestic customers also pushed the Japanese banks to look for external borrowers. Held back from such activities through most of the post-War period, the banks in the late 1970s dramatically increased their foreign solicitations of yen loans, as did institutional investors for yen private placements, using the slowly growing number of offshore branches and trips by Tokyo-based bankers. Table 9.1 shows the sharp jump in external deals which resulted. In 1976, only about ¥100 billion was lent abroad in the form of yen loans; no private placements were recorded. In calendar 1979, nearly ¥2 trillion of loans and private placements represented tapping by the rest of the world of a swollen Japanese money supply the authorities were trying to recycle.

Table 9.1
Japanese External Lending in Yen, 1976/79 (¥ billion)

Calendar year	Loans	Private placements
1966	100	0
1977	170	30
1978	880	105
1979	1,900	67.2

Source: Ministry of Finance International Finance Bureau, Planning Section

Distinction Between Loans and Private Placements

For non-resident borrowers, the Ministry of Finance makes a technical distinction between a private placement and a loan; as the former is considered a step towards a public offering, the issuer, size of issue and timing are carefully monitored. Lenders which may offer private placements are limited to 50 financial institutions, but these include all of the long-term banks, city banks, trust banks and large insurance houses; sources of direct loans are approximately the same. Loans involve routine approval, allow more flexible terms and are common for industrial borrowers. Publicly announced syndicated loans are another type of recycling, but generally used by government or government agencies.

As a rough comparison, usual terms of yen loans and private placements are as follows:

	Loan	Private Placement
Borrowers	Prime government or corporate credits	
Approval	Routine approval by MOF	Detailed approval by Securities Bureau of MOF. Notes not to be traded in secondary market until after two years.
Conversion	Proceeds generally to be converted shortly after issue into foreign currencies; some exceptions are made.	
Maximum amount	¥ 50 billion	¥ 15–20 billion
Maturities	5–20 years	5–15 years
Grace period	5–10 years	5–7 years
Prepayments	Permitted; penalty fee to be negotiated.	Not during grace period; thereafter at 2% or 3% and sliding in annual decreases of $\frac{1}{2}$% to $\frac{1}{4}$%.
Rate	Fixed, or floating at a premium over long-term prime.	Fixed
Costs	Negotiable: from nil from single lender to $\frac{3}{4}$% for syndications, small stamp tax.	1% flat
Documentation	Similar to Euro-currency transactions.	International practice; agent bank named (more cumbersome than loans).

Recycling Nature

In late 1979 and early 1980, the recycling nature of yen lending abroad was again manifested. The poor performance of the Japanese Balance of Payments after the second oil shock caused real concern in Tokyo, particularly as the WPI increased at double digit annual rates during the period. The fall of the yen exacerbated the problem; despite $8 billion or so of intervention in 1979, the authorities were not able to bring the yen back to their apparent goal of 200. Several steps were taken to complement market intervention: cancellation of the samurai leasing programme,[1] reduction of the "emergency" import programme and repeated raising of interest rates. The tap, in effect, was turned off.

Yen availability to non-residents was clearly again—as it always had been—a function of the Balance of Payments position of Japan, since the granting of yen credit in any form deteriorates the basic balance and weakens the spot yen after conversion of the proceeds. A correlation can be seen graphically in Table 9.2, which also shows the lag effect before official policy responds to Balance of Payments trends.

Table 9.2
Correlation of Balance of Payments Current Account with External Yen Loans, 1976/79

	Current account ($ billion)		Yen loans to non-residents (¥ billion)
1976	3,680	1977	200
1977	10,918	1978	985
1978	16,534	1979	1,967.2
1979	(8,750)	Fy 1980[E]	250

Source: Nomura Research Institute

Aggregation of Yen Credits

A further constraint on the availability of yen to non-residents is the aggregation of yen loans of domestic banks. Yen credits of all types—domestic, interbank, foreign—are lumped together and subjected to official guidance in the form of a quarterly ceiling for each bank. To the extent that Japan-based banks experience difficulty in meeting the credit demands of their domestic customers, foreign borrowers will take second place. At times of severe credit restriction (which will correspond with increased yen interest costs), it may become difficult to negotiate any type of yen credit to non-residents, owing to the natural tendency of Japan's banks to help first their group or other local companies. Foreign bank branches in Tokyo are similarly affected; foreign-owned subsidiaries may find it hard to obtain credit as a result. This ordering of priorities by Japanese lenders is quite natural; it complements and accentuates the direction of the authorities concerning the volume of foreign yen loans. In late 1979, for example, both tightening credit ceilings and official discouragement of all but a small category of yen loans to non-residents coincided.

Conversion of Proceeds

Similarly, the instructions concerning the conversion of proceeds of yen loans to external borrowers will follow the official policy *vis-à-vis* balance of payments. If recycling of surplus inflows is desired, quick conversion of yen credits will be required; if the opposite, yen borrowers may keep the proceeds in Tokyo for longer periods. On-lending to subsidiaries in Japan would usually be possible in the second situation, unlikely to be permitted in the first.

The Export-Import Bank as a Source of Funds

The Export-Import Bank of Japan provides both suppliers' credits for Japanese exporters and direct loans to foreign governments and corporations for equipment and services from Japan. The former category also includes import credit and overseas investment credit to Japanese international companies expanding abroad. Buyers' credits are, so far, made only in yen and tend to be directed to government entities or foreign banks, rather than commercial firms. A buyer's credit would likely include the following terms:

Amount available:	(100%)
down payment	15–20%
financed by buyer	10%
financed by ExIm and	70% (of which EIBJ takes 70%)
Japanese banks	
Tenor	10 years
Rate	Fixed
Guarantee	L/C or L/G from foreign bank

Dollar Loans

Strictly speaking, dollar loans made by Japanese banks are *not* part of tapping the Japanese reservoir. Japanese dollar reserves—for the most part—are not channelled to the Japanese banks for on-lending (or undercutting their rivals) abroad. Some deposits are given to Japanese and foreign banks in Tokyo, but the great bulk of Japanese dollar reserves is held in U.S. government instruments in America.

Dollar deals—whether syndicated loans or private placements—are not commonly negotiated or booked in Tokyo, where offshore transactions are blocked by tax and other regulations. Such loans are put together, or joined into, by the London and New York offices of Japanese banks, competing with Western rivals. Dollar or other currencies are funded by the banks from foreign sources: interbank deposits, deposits at branches, CDs, FRNs, etc.

Official guidance is again felt, as the MOF extends its control over Japanese bank activity throughout the world. In October 1979, for example, the MOF radically reduced the participation of Japanese banks in offshore dollar deals abroad by (1) imposing a more rigorous ratio for matching medium-term foreign currency assets with medium-term liabilities; (2) introducing a formula for country risk—20% of equity to any one sovereign credit—and (3) sharply discouraging Japanese banks from increasing their foreign currency loans.

Some observers feel that the authorities may be over-stepping their bounds in this area. Dollar loans funded and left offshore do not touch the Japanese economy nor affect the capital reservoir. Balance of Payments flows (except for a concomitant increase in invisible earnings) are unaffected. The MOF is acting here in its role as controller of the banking system, looking at prudential ratios, profitability and possible funding difficulties. It has also often tried to blunt criticism, for example, of the reputation of Japanese banks that they were undermining the European markets by cut-rate deals. Some transactions came to be known as *kamikaze* loans; the efforts of MOF to prevent these criticisms also stifled the natural desire of Japanese banks to grow internationally, to gain expertise, and to augment domestic assets with international ones.

International market makers have been confused by this policy. While occasionally complaining about "dumping", most Western banks have welcomed the important participation of Japanese lenders in the medium-term syndicated loans now necessary to keep many less-developed countries afloat. An on-again, off-again approach, not knowing whether Japanese banks will play an important role in any credits, has made their structuring more difficult.

Don't Count on Yen Availability

Thus, the Japanese capital reservoir is growing and often liquid. Sometimes the tap is turned on and credits in yen flow. At other times, official attitudes freeze the reservoir and turn off the tap. While on balance and over time, a useful addition to world liquidity is growing in Japan, foreign borrowers cannot count on access to it at any one given time.

NOTE

1. This programme offered cheap dollar financing for the purchase of airplane and other large capital items by Japanese lessors, which simultaneously leased them to outside users. The purchase was counted as "imports" in Balance of Payments accounting.

CHAPTER 10

Samurai Bonds

The other portion of the capital reservoir of Japan which can be tapped by foreign borrowers is the long-term yen bond market. Bonds issued by non-residents in the local yen market have come to be known as *samurai bonds*, in direct analogy to the "Yankee" bonds issued by non-residents in the N.Y. dollar market. This source has been opened to corporations after years of debate, and can be considered a new opportunity to raise capital. However, the new source can be turned off at any time by the Japanese authorities, again in correlation with external economic policy concerning the Balance of Payments.

The Japanese Bond Market

The development of Japanese primary and secondary bond markets has paralleled the economic growth of Japan itself.[1] If all types of bonds are included, the primary issuing sector reached about $100 billion in annual new issue amount in 1980. Growth in the volume of primary issues is shown in Table 10.1.

The most interesting feature of that table is the growth of public debt issues: in FY 1979, the deficit of the central government of Japan amounted to ¥15 trillion, or about $70 billion, an amount equal to the combined deficits of the U.S., U.K., Germany and France in the same period.

Principal issuers of domestic bonds, besides central and local government, in Japan include:

— long-term banks;
— the Bank of Tokyo;
— large electric power companies; and
— industrial entities.

Both public issues and private placements are present; the major intermediaries, either as underwriters or agents in private placements, are the 14 major securities firms entitled to be managing underwriters. The "Big Four" dominate the Japanese bond (and stock) markets; Table 10.2 shows their respective positions in order of selected bonds underwritten in FY 1979.

Table 10.1
Primary Issue Volume
Japan Domestic Bond Market, FY 1974/80
(¥ billion)

FY	Private sector	Public sector	Total	Public sector as % of total
1974	7,818	7,482	15,300	48.9
1975	11,086	9,877	20,963	47.1
1976	10,758	13,770	24,528	56.1
1977	12,383	17,115	29,498	58.0
1978	13,675	19,394	33,069	58.6
1979	13,689	21,513	35,201	61.1
1980	5,746	30,163	35,909	84.0

Source: Nomura Research Institute

With this volume of activity and large capital funds of their own, the "Big Four" come under careful government scrutiny and influence. Their functions, especially selection of borrowers, timing and rates, are in large part set by government policy, not market conditions. It is customary for top Bank of Japan and Ministry of Finance officials, upon retirement to become advisers to or executives of the "Big Four", complementing the co-operation between market movers and government policy.

Investors in the primary bond market include banks, other financial institutions such as savings and co-operative banks, insurance companies, and individual subscribers. Until the mid-sixties, bonds were purchased mostly by banks, especially city banks, but recently the percentage of individual subscribers has increased. A major feature of the primary bond market is the forced purchase of government securities by Japanese banks, as described above. Accounting for such bond holdings when interest rates are rising has hurt the operating results of the city banks in recent years, while purchase of new issues has forced sales of existing holdings in the secondary market.[2]

Table 10.2
Role of the "Big Four" Securities Houses
FY 1979 Yen Issues Underwritten
(¥ billion)

	Samurai bonds (Public issues)		10-year government bonds	
	Number	Amount	Amount	% of national total
Nomura	7	135	481.6	43.98
Nikko	2	46	119.8	10.94
Daiwa	2	48	119.8	10.94
Yamaichi	3	55	119.8	10.94

Source: Nomura Research Institute

Origins of the Samurai Market

Until 1970, no foreign entities of any kind were permitted to issue bonds in Japan. By that year, Japan had turned from a capital-importing country to one with a surplus Balance of Payments position and an increased perception of its international commitments. Japanese investors were given permission to buy foreign securities (with prior approval case by case). In November 1970, the first issuer, the Asian Development Bank (ADB) was permitted to offer yen denominated bonds to Japanese investors. The Asian Development Bank was not a surprising first choice, as this Manila-based development organisation is very heavily supported by Japan, which provides 40% of its grant and inter-government loan funds, the Executive Director and a host of economists and lending officers. The ADB issue opened the floodgates and in the ensuing ten years many government or supra-government agencies have issued yen bonds, a total amount of over $6 billion. Issues per year and amounts are shown in Table 10.3.

Table 10.3
Samurai Bond Issues in Japan
1970/80
(¥ billion)

FY	Number	Total amount	All Japanese bond issues
1970	1	6	6258
1971	4	48	9026
1972	5	70	11,046
1973	3	40	13,029
1974	—	—	15,299
1975	3	35	20,963
1976	6	62	24,527
1977	22	454	29,498
1978	28	657	33,069
1979	14	284	35,201
1980	15	280	35,909

Source: Bond Underwriters Association of Japan and Nomura Research Institute

Outflows are again more graphic if compared to Japan's current account.

The lack of new issues in 1974 exactly correlates with the turn-around of Japan's Balance of Payments after the 1973/74 oil shock. The sharp fall-off of samurai bonds in late 1979 and 1980 reflected the same conditions.

Permission to issue samurai bonds is given by MOF under a queue system. Elements which MOF will take into account are BOP trends and the amount of liquidity in the national economy, i.e. , competing needs for yen funds from domestic borrowers, as well as political benefits. Typically, a quota per quarter is set for prospective issues; borrowers at the top of the queue fall naturally into the quota by rotation, if they agree with the underwriters on terms (there are cases, however, of queue jumping, based on political considerations).

Table 10.4
Samurai Bonds and Current Account Trends, 1969/80

Calendar Year	Japan's current account ($ million)	FY	Samurai bonds issued (¥ billion)
1969	2,119	1970	6
1970	1,970	1971	48
1971	5,797	1972	70
1972	6,624	1973	40
1973	(136)	1974	—
1974	(4,693)	1975	35
1975	(682)	1976	62
1976	3,680	1977	454
1977	10,918	1978	657
1978	16,534	1979	284
1979	(8,750)	1980	280

A further look at Table 10.3 shows the relative volume of samurai bonds. In no single year from 1970 to 1976 did samurai bonds approach 1/10% of all new issues in Japan; in 1977, 1978 and 1979, respectively, samurai bonds accounted for a markedly higher percentage. Liquidity *per se* is not the major consideration; in Japan, the state of the current account and political ties with the borrower (or borrower's country) are more germane.

For borrowers, availability of credit, interest rate advantages and the current and expected values of the yen become decisive elements. Impediments to bond issuance are problems such as *"crowding out"*—lack of absorption in the bond markets due to other contemporary issuers. In late 1979, for instance, the need to expand government bond issues to cover Japan's budget deficit was a second factor behind the throttling down of samurai bonds to low levels.

Typical Conditions for Samurai Bonds

Term:	Until the five-year issue by Norway in 1978, all samurai bonds had maturities of ten years or more; more recently, five-year final maturities are more common.
Interest rates:	Fixed, and close to the prevailing long-term prime rate. There is little if any rate discrimination among borrowers.
Tax provisions:	Withholding tax is applicable, but is waived for foreign government purchases.
Allocation to non-residents:	25% of a primary issue of a samurai bond can be purchased by non-residents; no restrictions are placed on the secondary market, so that at

Listing:
Conversion of
proceeds:

times a higher percentage gravitates to foreign hands immediately after issue. (This is a countervailing element to the primary government goal of recycling Balance of Payments inflows and excessive liquidity.)
On the Tokyo Stock Exchange.
Since the primary object of the government in permitting samurai bonds is to recycle monetary flows and to lower the spot rate of the yen, conversion requirements have been strict. Borrowers' external surplus periods have only days or weeks in which to sell the yen proceeds and buy another currency. This is relaxed when Japan is in external deficit, but then issues themselves are curtailed. In many cases, this means a direct exchange risk, for the government agencies borrowing yen often have no yen income.

Advent of Corporate Samurai Bonds

A principal feature of samurai bonds is that they are unguaranteed, unsecured and have no pledged collateral, characteristic for issues of governments or supragovernmental agencies. A number of foreign corporations, attracted by availability and lower rates of yen bonds, made inquiries in the late 1970s about joining the queue, which faced MOF and the underwriters with a difficult precedent. No domestic corporate bonds in Japan were then issued without collateral or security of some kind. Foreign companies could hardly pledge foreign assets, nor would they be inclined to do so, coming from markets where such requirements were not found. To permit unsecured bond issues by foreign firms was to open an avenue which the regulatory authorities were not quite ready to explore.

Sears Roebuck, a "Triple A" firm of impeccable standing, finally was able to breach this particular wall with a samurai bond in March 1979, a five-year issue with no security. (Interestingly enough, Sears had no subsidiaries in Japan and no major trade generating yen receivables. Its borrowing was predicated on diversification of general borrowing requirements and the public relations value of being the first corporate samurai issuer.)

MOF thereupon formulated a policy that "Triple A"-rated firms would have access to the samurai market in the future, subject to the usual criteria of timing, queuing, etc. This would allow some 30 U.S. companies and additional firms in the EEC to consider samurais. Two Japanese companies were also publicly named as being able to issue bonds without collateral: Toyota and Matsushita Electric, premier names in Japan.

Yen Bonds in a World Context

A second measure of the growth of the Japanese bond market in world terms can be seen in Table 10.5.

Table 10.5
Growth of Yen Bonds, 1974/79

	1974	1975	1976	1977	1978	1979
Gross Euro-bond issues ($ billion)	3	11	15	19	16	18
Gross foreign bond issues ($ billion)	5	12	19	17	21	19
Yen bonds (¥ billion)	—	35	62	484	672	289
Yen bonds as %	1	1	1	4	13	7

Source: Nomura Research Institute

Clearly shown is the rapid growth of yen bonds when the gates were opened in late 1977/78, and the effect of their closing again in 1979/80.

Future Trends

Trends in the samurai bond market will depend on the following conditions:
— Japan's Balance of Payments outlook;
— Primary market capacity;
— The course of the yen;
— Ability to raise private placements;
— Development of the secondary market; and
— Political relations with prospective issuing governments.
The volume and timing of samurai bonds should continue to be a function of the *outlook for Japan's Balance of Payments.* It can be expected that when Japan has a pattern similar to the external deficits of 1979/80 and the yen is weak, capital outflows will be discouraged. When the opposite is true, as in 1977/78, samurai issues (as well as a concatenation of concocted gimmicks such as samurai leasing) will be encouraged.

Primary market capacity may interfere with potential samurai issues, even in the absence of external disequilibrium. Government deficits are likely, in the early 1980s, to be a feature of life in a Japan which is still woefully lacking in infrastructure, which faces secularly decreased growth and which still lacks a national social security system while its citizens have the longest life expectancy in the world.

The *strength of the yen* and expectations as to its further course will affect potential borrowers, particularly those which are using samurai bonds for general funding, rather than for matching long-term yen assets. When the yen is perceived to be momentarily weak, considerably less demand will be shown by borrowing entities which evaluate foreign exchange losses than in periods where the yen is felt to be overvalued. Of course, there will continue to be central governments concerned more with availability of funds than with foreign exchange losses, which may continue borrowing no matter what the yen rate outlook is.

Private placements in yen are a source of capital which competes with samurai bonds to tap the reservoir of Japanese liquidity. These also fall under the control of the monetary authorities: their availability likewise depends on the state of the Balance of Payments.

A *poor secondary market* has affected the samurai bond environment since its inception. The surfeit of bonds offered in the Japanese capital markets overall has often caused periods when the secondary market was effectively closed to samurai bonds. This reverberates in the primary market and can delay or impede issues.

The *relationship between Japan and the foreign governments* wishing to issue samurai bonds is a factor which may outweigh some of the economic and structural constraints outlined above. Despite the Tokyo authorities' wish to contain external monetary outflows at certain times, it can be difficult for them to deny access to the samurai bond market to major governments which have already borrowed in that market or wish to begin doing so. Given the repeated friction between Japan and many Western countries which, rightly or wrongly, accuse it of "dumping" its exports, Japan necessarily has to weigh carefully the further political implications of denying national governments access to its liquidity.

Conclusion

Samurai bonds should become available to more corporate borrowers and may offer at times a way to tap the yen reservoir at attractive nominal costs. But access to the reservoir will be controlled by the authorities for the indefinite future, since this device is perceived primarily by the Japanese authorities as a way to recycle Balance of Payments inflows and/or surplus liquidity in the domestic economy. The Ministry of Finance's International Bureau is interested in the diplomatic value of opening Japan's yen bond market to foreign governments and companies, but this desire is often diluted by the need to float massive amounts of government bonds to cover its own recurring deficits.

APPROACHING THE MINISTRY OF FINANCE

Seeking permission for external credits and a plethora of domestic activities means approaching the MOF for permission. *Companies* do not go directly to bureaux of the Ministry of Finance. For legal, administrative and tax matters, they are represented by professional advisers, occasionally lawyers or accountants. An elder statesman or retired diplomat may be used as intermediary. For financial transactions of all kinds, the company's bankers—

who will be carrying out the transaction and thus require explicit or implicit permission in most cases—will approach the relevant section. Selection of the right adviser/intermediary is critical in obtaining Ministry of Finance understanding and approval of investment, financing and other schemes.

For those directly involved with contacting the Ministry of Finance, the following guidelines are suggested:

Start at the right level. Decisions in Japan are typically made from the bottom up, not the top down. On important issues, middle levels coalesce to discuss the matter fully and present it higher up. "Superiors do not force their ideas on juniors—instead, juniors spontaneously lay their opinions before their superiors and have them adopted."[3]

Identify the right individual. Know who is presently responsible for the area concerned, or for passing on relevant requests further. Know where he stands in the hierarchy, and the powers of his section and bureau. Try to ascertain which other sections or bureaux may have a vested interest in the matter.

Analyse his perceptions. Is the matter administrative, or does it involve policy? Does its importance overlap with the probable values of the individual?

See your request's implications clearly, in terms of

— *National policy.* Where does the request fit in in terms of present national policies? It will be of little use for a foreign bank to go to the Ministry of Finance to ask for permission to issue yen bonds, if Japanese city banks themselves cannot do so. (However, foreign institutions can sometimes be used as vehicles to bring about new services, such as consumer finance, before Japanese ones do.)

— *Written or guidance orientations.* Is one asking the official to give you the written record of the law or his interpretation and guidance in one of the many areas where no written law exists? Is the request for information, advice, guidance or permission?

— *Competing interests.* Understand what similar requests competitors may have made, or what privileges they enjoy. However, to insist on fair play or extract similar treatment is often futile; Japanese officials give authorisation or largesse based on a complex variety of factors not necessarily based on visible fairness.

Analyse which other groups in the economy may have, or be asking for, similar privileges? What would granting the request mean to them? How will other sections of the Ministry of Finance respond to approval of the request?

Be logical. Unemotional and logical requests will receive commensurate treatment; aggressive Western insistence may result in stubborn refusal. This does not, however, rule out persistence, nor playing upon Japanese knowledge of the international issues involved with the foreign company's government.

Show the benefit to Japan. The most compelling reason for a Japanese government official to accede to a request is for the national interest to be involved. Emphasise the national context of the request and how the benefit to one company is also a benefit to Japan (benefits can be monetary, but also more ephemeral such as educational value).

Don't criticise the decision openly or publicly. By keeping a low profile, room for re-opening the matter, and compromise remains. There is great sensitivity to open criticism from Westerners; although an initial request may be granted, the hostility engendered thereafter may not be worth it.

Take a Japanese colleague along. Answers of Ministry of Finance officials may not be what they appear on the surface. A seemingly positive response can have negative implications, or an apparent turndown offer hints how to approach the problem or the bureau in a different way. For this reason, it is vital to have a Japanese officer of the company make the request or be present when the request is made. Similarly, indirect requests are better received than ones which are too blunt.

A Note on Stock Listing

A handful of Western companies have attempted to raise funds in Japan by listing on the Tokyo stock market. At the time of writing, 17 companies—14 U.S., two French, one Dutch—had listed their shares. (Two have delisted since the initial flurry in 1973 and 1974.) Listing costs are not onerous: for a company with paid-up capital of $1 billion, initial listing costs would be around ¥50 million. These attempts have apparently not yet proven very successful. The performance of foreign shares on the Tokyo Stock Exchange has been poor in yen terms, since the dollar has depreciated sharply against the yen and the N.Y. Dow Jones Index has stagnated for a decade when the Tokyo market was steadily rising. Little interest in buying shares has come from the Japanese public and the exercise must be seen more as a public relations one than an attempt to raise capital.

NOTES

1. An excellent description of this area can be found in Nomura Securities: *An Introduction to the Japanese Bond Market*, Tokyo, Sept. 1978, and Industrial Bank of Japan: *Handbook of the Japanese Bond Market:* Tokyo, 1979.

92

2. See "Issuance of a Large Volume of Public Bonds and its Effects on Bank Management", *Sanwa Economic Letter*, March 1978.
3. Chie Nakane. *Japanese Society*, Berkeley: University of California Press, 1970, p. 65.

B. Financial Management

CHAPTER 11

Cash Management in Japan

The goals of domestic cash management are much the same in every country: optimal use of financial resources, protection against exchange losses and minimisation of external borrowing. In Japan, cash management is influenced by the different approach to bank relationships outlined in previous chapters, and impeded by a lack of instruments for refining net asset and liability positions.

Japanese corporations are aware of the mathematical benefits of good cash management. Yet, as a general statement, bank relationship factors outweigh the maximisation of cash management gains for Japanese firms. Bank relationships are usually seen as more important than cash management because bank loans replace more normal equity accounts of Western companies. To avoid the possibility of unavailability of credit in the future, financial executives in Japan have been willing to negotiate more credit lines than required, maintain compensating balances which are larger than necessary, and increase those balances as effective interest yields go up although nominal rates do not. This is found in arrangements based on both the short and long-term prime rates. Total effective interest costs may not be identified.

Foreign companies, however, are not as bound—should not accept being bound—by such constraints; they must be aware of local bank relationship factors, but should negotiate precise effective rates and keep unutilised balances to a minimum. Indeed, their goal in Japan should be to adopt the "zero balance" approach customary in the West. Reduction of excess unutilised cash will be hampered by limitations of the market, but this position has been achieved by a number of Western firms in Japan. (Some Japanese companies are coming around to this way of thinking, as their own equity accounts and liquidity wax and dependence on banks wanes.) The following sections give a step-by-step analysis of the components of domestic cash management and their relevance to Japanese-based firms.

THE COLLECTION PROCESS

Domestic cash management can be divided into three distinct stages: collections, treasury management and disbursements. While the outer stages are mechanical and semi-automatic, they are used to maximise amounts of funds for treasury management, which concentrates on their optional deployment.

It is instructive to divide these steps further. The collection process, for example, can be broken into distinct areas, as shown in Figure 11.1.

Japan offers a number of ways to optimise collections, through nation-wide bank systems and excellent computer-based money transfer methods; there is also excellent customer adherence to credit terms. The collection process in a Japanese setting takes into account the different instruments and business patterns prevailing, as shown below.

Order and Invoice Systems

The first step of cash management is an internal one: check if the billing procedure used gives unnecessary delays or inadvertent credit extension. For example, if credit terms are stated to be "X days from the date of invoice" and invoice creation is delayed after shipment, that delay is given to customers as free credit; this is more costly if a week-end is involved. Even if month-end terms are included, late invoicing can dip over a month-end and allow greater credit to buyers. But these are not uniquely Japanese problems. Since month-end terms are common in Japan, only minor care need be given to assure that statements are created simultaneously with shipment.

Customer Payment Methods

More important is the way in which Japanese customers are asked to pay, as there are three basic non-cash methods they can use, each with implications for the collection period:
— sending in a promissory note;
— using a bank transfer; or
— sending their own cheque.

Promissory notes

Sending a promissory note is the most common method used by business firms in settling accounts, particularly for inventory purchases. The maturity of these notes is usually 60–90 days; they are sent to the supplier upon receipt of its statement. Payment of such notes is effected through the national clearing system, as are other instruments. The notes are paid at due date and represent an excellent cash collection tool.

Receipt of a promissory note—in effect a bill of exchange—can be used to develop financing for the supplier. The seller can discount the note at its house bank, endorse it to a third party or use notes as collateral for advances or overdrafts from its banks. The two-name nature of the paper adds to the security and makes financing easier to obtain. Stamp tax applies.

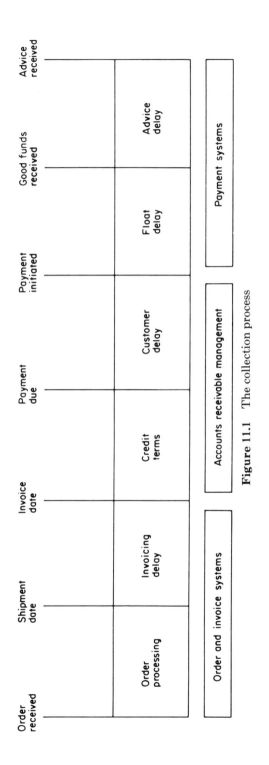

Figure 11.1 The collection process

Bank transfers

It is not surprising that Japan has a fully integrated telecommunications system, offering computer-assisted bank transfers. The nation-wide system is bolstered by equivalent internal communications in each bank. Very rapid transfers are possible, as shown below:

Transfers	Same bank	Between banks
Within Tokyo	Same day	Same day
Between two cities	Same or next day	Next day

"Urgent" remittance methods can also be used; these accelerate advice of a payment, which can be handled within a single day, even between two distant cities. The charge for accelerated transfers is ¥500; according to the amount (or the credit concern), a standard break-even amount can be set for automatic use of such transfers by comparing that cost with the yield on funds available earlier.

Cheques

Large companies do not typically use cheques in paying their bills, although smaller ones may. Firms dealing with retail outlets, individuals, clinics, etc. will often receive cheques, collected and deposited by their salesmen and messengers. Here, the value dating is:

— Cheque presented to bank of drawer

	Same branch	Another branch
	One day	Two days

— Cheque presented to bank of drawee

	Same city as drawer	Different cities
	Two days	Three–four days

If cheques are mailed to the supplier, further float delays can be expected.

Direct debiting

There is a legal basis for direct debiting in Japan, which is rather widely used by utilities. Many firms and individuals are debited directly in their bank accounts under prior written agreement. This method has not yet been used by private commercial firms, owing to the fact that alternative methods are quick and payment dates well respected.

Customer Payment Habits

Japanese suppliers enjoy both prompt and full payment by customers. In a country where social acceptance and good standing as a member of the community are all-important, there are strong pressures on firms to maintain payment integrity. Most people routinely pay for month-end settlement on the 25th of each month; the streets of Tokyo are even more jammed than usual between the 25th and 30th each month by company cars going around to pick up cash and cheques from customers. Customers are amenable to changing payment instructions to help the supplier, if this costs them nothing; average bad debt losses are extremely low.

Guidelines for Collection Management

Account receivable collection, therefore, should not present a serious problem to the well-organised firm in Japan. If correctly arranged, a company's collections can be set up in a virtually automatic way and float reduced to a minimum. The following points should be studied:
— Is inadvertent credit given to customers by slow billing?
— Do discounts offered reflect the true value of funds invested or costs saved from reduced borrowing?
— Are clear instructions given to customers as to payment method?
— Can a single city bank's network be used to collect, and then concentrate inflows?
— Are salesmen or messengers, who pick up cash and cheques, depositing these receipts in the most efficient manner?
— Is the best use being made of computerised bank transfer possibilities?
— Are inflows directed to banks where overdraft lines are maintained, so that net borrowing is reduced?

TREASURY MANAGEMENT

This area can be more frustrating. There are not enough borrowing instruments to allow fine-tuning of cash control as in the West (although this is improving) and investment media are limited. Furthermore, as the preceding chapters have shown, interest rates for both assets and liabilities are set or influenced directly by the government, often making them artificially high or low.

Borrowing

A standard technique for companies in Western markets is to try to keep their unutilised cash balances at zero. Surplus cash is immediately invested or used to bring down borrowings. This kind of technique requires very short-term instruments on both sides. In Japan, the standard borrowing technique is to discount promissory notes or to take out credit advances, both for usual periods of 90 days. These "evergreen" credits may not fit perfectly with the company's cash flow. Individually seen, this means that a company may have to borrow in blocs of funds corresponding with its highest peak daily need, maintaining unnecessarily high borrowings thereafter. It is possible to negotiate overdrafts within a given month but much more difficult over a month-

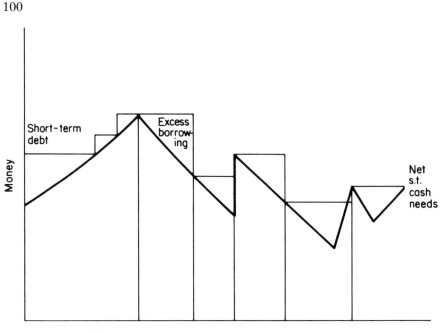

Figure 11.2. Effect of borrowing "blocs" of funds

end, particularly quarter-end, because Japanese banks often fall under credit ceiling controls. The inherent unpredictability of overdraft usage is a distinct handicap to Japanese banks, as they may not know the amounts of overdrafts extended until the day after the quarter-end and thus be over their credit ceiling. Furthermore, banks benefit from the higher average borrowings outstanding inherent in a system of three-month loans. Overdrafts, however, are easier to negotiate from foreign banks in Japan and there are foreign companies which have been able to come close to a zero balance approach by a combination of long-term loans for basic investment, short-term loans for import and working capital financing and overdrafts to top up their local requirements. Several international oil companies in particular have reached this structure.

Complicating the issue is, of course, the area of compensating balances. The Japanese banks' predilection for lower nominal rates and larger compensating balances runs counter to good cash management. Cash management is constrained by target levels of compensating balances, which, even if only loosely expressed, are meant to be steadily held.

Short-term Investment

Traditionally, there have been only three types of investment media available in Japan: bank deposits, short-term treasury bills and *gensaki* (repurchase arrangements with a security house). *Bank deposits* have interest rates fixed by the authorities at low levels to avoid competition with the Postal Savings System. These deposits cannot be broken (although they can be counted as compensating balances). *Treasury bills* offer better interest rates and there is a secondary market for such instruments. However, their tenors are only 60–64 days and there are periods of time when neither primary nor secondary issues of these instruments are available to the investor, limiting them as a major instrument.

Gensaki were formerly frowned on by the government, as this grey market appeared to offer an escape from monetary supply control in times of credit restriction. In 1979, the government's wish to sponsor inflows of capital opened the yen *gensaki* market to foreigners for the first time, effectively giving it official recognition. *Gensaki* rates are set by supply and demand and often offer the highest level of return. (They also can be used as a borrowing source if the company has adequate securities of its own.) *Gensaki* deals can range between as short as a few days to as long as several months.

Certificates of deposits (CDs) were permitted in 1979. Japanese banks were allowed to issue CDs up to 25% of their capital, foreign banks up to 10% of their yen loans and investments. The market appeal was limited to larger investors, since the minimum amount was ¥500 million; CD tenors were three to six months. Despite these restrictions, certificates of deposit are an important new instrument. Supply and demand set their interest rates, which are an accurate reflection of market forces. Foreign entities may purchase certificates of deposit; several central banks have done so in their portfolio diversification efforts.

A broad secondary market, however, has yet to appear. Certificates of deposit, under present law, are not freely transferable bearer instruments; changes in ownership must be physically recorded. To make certificates of deposit a truly flexible investment medium, and a better funding source for banks, existing law would have to be changed for certificates of deposit to be bearer instruments. Securities firms would then develop a true secondary market. No limits should apply on tenor or size of yen certificates of deposit, and, ideally, banks should be given latitude to issue them at their discretion.

More effective use of compensating balances can be seen as an investment medium. Higher percentages of compensating balances held in interest-bearing time deposits, rather than non-interest-bearing current accounts, are feasible; banks are not always insistent on exact mathematical trade-off of different interest-bearing accounts. If both cash flow and interest rate projections of the company have been accurate enough over time, it may keep average balances at the level negotiated, but maintain higher current account deposits when interest rates are down, lower ones where they are higher.

Pooling

Pooling is not a standard technique as it is restricted by the legal framework, which does not permit the use of an account by more than one account holder. However, the goal of "pooling"—using the cash flows of two or more related companies to minimise borrowing or maximise invested funds—still may apply. In some countries in the West, this is accomplished by joint accounts or by automatic transfers daily into or out of a mutual short-term investment account. Somewhat the same effect can be achieved by negotiating with a bank in Japan to count the balances of one group member as compensating balances toward the requirements of another. Foreign banks will be more receptive to this than local ones.

DISBURSEMENTS

Optimising disbursement management implies accruing payment float to the paying company. The question of using float to one's own advantage is a delicate one. As the Japanese have precise payment habits, it would be possible for a foreign company to suffer a loss of reputation were it to practice too aggressively types of payment deceleration common in the West. While float could be obtained by, for example, writing cheques drawn on a bank in Hokkaido, this would be seen as an aberration and could hurt the company's relationship with its suppliers. It is inadvisable to build in float payments to suppliers as part of the local cash management cycle. More important to consider are the following questions:
— Is the Disbursement Section fully aware of cash management objectives for the company?
— Are discounts offered adequately evaluated and accepted?
— Does the same flexibility exist for disbursement in connection with bank lines as for collections?, i.e., are there enough overdraft facilities in place to allow disbursements to be maximised, particularly taking into account discounts?
— Are minimum compensating balances in banks co-ordinated with disbursement schedules?

EXPORT COLLECTION

Exchange control has been liberalised in Japan, but export collection management remains predicated on the fundamental methods used, typically letters of credit and documentary collections. Use of standard banking instruments affects the ability to maximise export collections. Such instruments are handled in a standard way throughout the world and the problem of Japan-based exporters in receiving inflows more quickly is like that of exporters in any other country.

Retained foreign currency accounts

For the company with two-way flows of foreign currency, an optimal technique is to maintain a foreign currency account into which receipts are credited and from which disbursements in foreign currency are made. These accounts are best located in major international banks in the financial centre of the country whose currency is involved. For example, retained currency accounts in dollars are more efficient when kept in major U.S. cities with money market banks.

This opportunity has recently become available for Japanese-based companies, which may now maintain such accounts abroad with Ministry of Finance license and put into them their export proceeds. Conversely, they may also open accounts at home in foreign currency with Japanese-based banks for the same purpose without any license. Settlement arrangements are tied in with these accounts, i.e. dollar export proceeds under letters of credit where the opening bank is in Japan can be directed to an account held in New York City. The trend towards more and more open account transactions, particularly intercompany ones, increases the attractiveness of using the same multinational banks in a number of market centres. *Netting* of intracompany receivables, however, is still considered an abnormal settlement method under the new exchange control system, and requires a Ministry of Finance license. So far, full multilateral netting has not been approved for Japanese multinationals or foreign subsidiaries operating in Japan.

CHAPTER 12

Foreign Exchange Exposure Management

Foreign exchange exposure management, as the author has pointed out,[1] requires a co-ordinated, centralised and sequential approach. This basic approach is as applicable in Japan as elsewhere; perceptions of foreign exchange exposure and the instruments with which to cover unacceptable risks in this area, however, differ.

The management of foreign exchange risk begins with definition of exposure, which is largely determined by the accounting conventions of the home country. Beyond the purely accounting exposure expressed in consolidation of balance sheets and other financial statements lie transaction and economic exposure of a longer range nature. Japanese companies tend to concentrate on the latter two types of exposure, for their own rules concerning consolidation are weaker than **"Generally Accepted Accounting Principles" (GAAP)** in, say, the U.S.A. and their attitudes to published results do not coincide with those of most Western companies.

After defining exposures theoretically, the multinational company faces the problem of *identifying* its individual positions at risk, both present and future. This area of identification is followed by *risk assessment*: the comparison of possible future rate changes with internal positions to determine the worst possible outcomes on an after-tax basis. This will weigh the potential impact on a firm's financial statements and its substance; the firm's own attitude to risk will determine which positions are unacceptable.

The next step in decision-making is to develop a *covering strategy*, utilising both internal and external hedging techniques. The organisational structure to accomplish that, in conjunction with liquidity management and tax planning, will be *centralised* and *anticipatory*, based on a treasury-oriented reporting system and centralised decision-making.

This conceptual approach to exchange risk management is valid in Japan and to Japanese companies. The following chapter therefore deals with the same sequence: the Japanese accounting background, Japanese attitude to risk and internal or external hedging techniques permitted.

The Accounting Background

The authoritative accounting body in Japan is the Japanese Institute of

Certified Public Accountants, which publishes general guidelines for accounting disclosure, including consolidation and translation of income. The presently valid standard for consolidation is the *Financial Accounting Standard on Consolidated Financial Statements*, promulgated by the Business Accounting Deliberation Council of the Ministry of Finance. The MOF sets guidelines in conjunction with the Institute and MOF's directions will directly influence companies' choice of accounting principles.

GAAP in Japan are roughly modelled along U.S. lines, but in *consolidation* of subsidiaries into a parent balance sheet allow more freedom than does the U.S. Financial Accounting Standards Board. The only mention of consolidation of foreign subsidiaries in the Japanese standard cited above is that "Translation of financial statements of a foreign subsidiary expressed in a foreign currency should be made in accordance with the standard practice generally accepted as fair and reasonable". Consolidation rules governing foreign subsidiaries of Japan-based firms allow the parent to account for ventures which amount to less than 10% of total assets on an equity basis, regardless of the percentage owned. Companies owning less than 50% are also carried on an equity basis, which has caused companies to sell parts of majority-owned subsidiaries to come below that limit. The buyers are often members of the same group. There can therefore be large differences between the ways a Japanese firm presents its balance sheet in Japan and for S.E.C. purposes.

The treatment of *reserves* is also noteworthy. Reserves can be built up in Japanese firms for possible foreign exchange losses. These can be voluntary reserves, created through appropriation of retained earning, or less commonly, through charges to operations. There is a more formal category: the "reserve for development of overseas markets", which is tax-deductible and ranges from 0.5% to 0.9% of the proceeds of allowed transactions. The treatment of *income* received in foreign currency is straightforward, being translated at average rates of the period. As in other countries, taxation of foreign exchange gains and losses depends on their nature. Translation losses are not tax-deductible, nor are unrealised translation gains taxable. Actual changes in cash flows from transaction losses or gains reduce or increase reported taxable income directly.

Japanese Attitudes to Foreign Exchange Risk

As described above, Japanese companies are often held by a tighter group of shareholders than elsewhere and are intertwined closely with their banks. Foreign exchange losses from translation—when not avoided anyway—are commonly considered of less importance than transaction losses. Many Japanese MNCs will admit privately to taking no cover for consolidation risks; virtually all are concerned to offset transaction exposure. Their attitude diverges quite sharply from that of U.S. treasurers in the period 1976/80, when FASB-8 in its original version was in effect. Under its former ruling, exchange gains or losses on translation/consolidation were taken directly into income quarterly, distorting EPS ratios and earnings trends unless exchange cover was taken in the market to offset accounting effects.

Japanese companies also prefer to avoid publishing exchange losses, even if of the ephemeral and often unmeaningful translation type, if cost factors are acceptable or manipulation is applicable. As one prominent accounting firm has pointed out, "Many Japanese companies have long strings of subsidiaries. In the absence of a requirement for consolidated financial statements, manipulation to improve earnings is possible, provided companies have different closing dates. Such devices as selling at arranged prices, unloading inventory, allocating administrative charges or overheads, declaring or withholding dividends and similar 'window dressing' devices are possible". [2]

Window dressing is prevalent in Japan and it is not surprising that "manipulation" is carried out in the exchange risk accounting area. Foreign-owned subsidiaries and joint ventures have no motivation to do so, as they fall under accounting standards of their parent company and do not generally disclose financial statements.

Even full consolidation requirements along U.S. lines may not be sufficient to disclose fully the true operating results of large Japanese companies. Robert Ballon states:

> "Japan's large trading companies are unique in terms of size, world-wide operations, diversification and integration of product lines. Consolidation would not be enough to provide truly meaningful statements. What would be necessary in addition, would be that financial statements of the parent and main subsidiaries be presented individually as well as by line of business. A herculean task indeed! And even if this were done, who among the investors, especially among the general investing public, would have the time, the energy or the expertise to read such statements?" [3]

"Gains" and "Losses" from Hedging

An anomaly can arise in the way in which Japanese MNCs report their interim results, including foreign exchange movements. "Losses" may be reported when there is a difference between the maturity rate of a forward contract used to hedge, say, export receipts and the actual spot exchange rate of that date. For example, the large consumer electric goods companies in Japan, heavily dependent on dollar exports, began to hedge their expected dollar receipts for the fall of 1979 by selling them forward several months before. They thereby assured themselves of yen/dollar conversion rates of around ¥218-220, a sensible and commendable policy in a time of extreme uncertainty in the foreign exchange markets. Furthermore, it was widely known that such companies could export profitably at yen rates of ¥210 or higher. Yet the newspapers carried articles such as "Sony loses ¥60 billion in foreign exchange" after the six-month closing date of 30 September 1979. These losses were nothing more than the difference between the final spot rate of ¥230-240 and that of the contracted forward sales, a classic misunderstanding of the concept of loss and hedging. The finance managers of such firms, who apparently came in for criticism from their Boards of Directors, were in the same position as airline executives, criticised for having insured their planes in a year when they had no crashes.

HEDGING: EXTERNAL

The chief external tools used to cover exposed positions by multinational companies are:
— Forward exchange contracts;
— Foreign currency loans;
— Discount/sale of foreign currency receivables;
— Retained currency accounts;
— Liability assumptions;
— Borrowing/deposit arrangements in two currencies;
— Export risk guarantees;
— Factoring; and
— Leasing.

Most of these are available in Japan to resident companies; they are discussed in turn below.

Forward exchange contracts

There are no limitations on a resident company entering into forward sale or purchase of a currency if it has a recorded underlying transaction. This can be as rudimentary as a cable from a foreign supplier stating that goods have been shipped—crude oil from the Arabian Gulf, for example. Expected but unbooked and unauthenticated receipts or disbursements, however, cannot be sold or purchased forward.

Assuming there is a recorded foreign currency commitment, the resident company can sell (or buy) its obligation forward for the maturity date, in the Tokyo exchange market or abroad (the latter is discouraged.) Quotes are readily made for dollar/yen deals to one year, less so for two years, but possible to obtain for up to five years through a few specialised banks. Optional contracts are available, as in other markets. Spreads are negotiable, but may range around 40 basis points over inter-bank forward rates.

Foreign currency loans

Impact loans are now largely used for foreign exchange hedging purposes. After the scrapping of formal foreign exchange control in 1980, foreign currency can be borrowed by resident companies without prior permission. Traditionally over three years in maturity, short-term impact loans of 3–12 months were introduced in 1979. At the time of writing, there is no restriction as to maturity or currency of such loans. The old unwritten restriction against foreign-owned companies taking down impact loans appears to have been lifted. (Until 1979 virtually no foreign-owned entity or even a joint venture could borrow impact loans, two exceptions being Caterpillar Mitsubishi and Kirin Seagram.) Impact loans have recently been done in:

— U.S. dollars
— Euro-sterling
— Euro-Swiss francs
— Domestic S.F.
— Euro-D.M.
— Euro-Norwegian kroner
— Bahraini dinars
— Kuwaiti dinars
— Saudi riyals

There is no reason, if funding is available to the banks which act as principals in such loans, for other currencies not to be available. Depending on the currency, impact loans are available at fixed or floating rates. Some have bullet maturities, other regular amortisation after an initial grace period. Most impact loans these days are unguaranteed; a few remain guaranteed by Japanese banks, or by parent companies. The foreign exchange conversion of the borrowed currency into yen at inception, and the reverse at maturity, is typically done by the lending bank on guaranteed loans.

An important innovation is the advent of multi-currency options. At a given period before rollover date, regardless of the initial currency, the borrower may elect one of several other Euro-currencies to replace the one originally borrowed. Such flexibility can be particularly important in foreign exchange management, permitting currency changes as a company's exposures move away from existing ones at the time of drawdown (it also allows speculation). Documentation is simple and straightforward.

Impact loans can foster *exchange netting*: the matching of one currency receipt with an obligation in another currency expected to move in parallel fashion. Dutch guilders could be borrowed, for instance, to cover a receivable in Deutsche marks. Some Japanese companies have borrowed currencies, such as the Kuwaiti dinar—in which they had no receipts—where there was a lower interest rate than dollars, to hedge dollar receivables in the thought that the Kuwaiti dinar would move roughly with the U.S. dollar over time.

Discount/sale of foreign currency receivables

There is less ability to discount or sell foreign currency paper arising from receivables. While the dollar bankers' acceptance market is quite large, both in use by direct importers and by Japanese banks, the mechanism of discounting foreign currency receivables is not well developed. More typical is to borrow foreign currency on a clean impact loan basis.

Retained currency accounts

After the liberalisation of exchange control, retained foreign currency accounts have become of considerable importance to internationally involved companies in Japan. Exporters may leave foreign currency receipts in accounts in Japan or abroad, to anticipate future disbursements in those currencies. Not only is foreign exchange risk reduced, but also some foreign exchange conversions are eliminated.

Liability assumptions

A liability assumption is used by a company to rid itself of a foreign currency debt by transferring it to another company. The technique is simple, both conceptually and administratively. Typically, a commercial bank as intermediary will find another company willing to take over a foreign currency loan from the borrower at an agreed-upon rate, probably for its own hedging purposes. The difference between original price and rate and present market conditions is open to negotiation. The intermediary bank receives a commission, usually from both sides. This technique is allowed in Japan, remains confidential and can be attractive to both parties.

Borrowing/deposit arrangements in two currencies

Another risk-avoiding possibility for importers in Japan owing foreign currency is to borrow yen, use the proceeds to buy the foreign currency spot and place them on deposit. On a straight cost basis, this should work out about as favourably as straight cover through forward contracts, but the imperfect Japanese exchange markets can allow a more advantageous cost structure. For example, forward import cover in D.M. for six months might cost 3.1% p.a. if a forward contract were taken out. If the borrowing/deposit scheme were used, a lower cost might be achieved.

More problematic is the attitude of the Japanese authorities. The above technique involves leading a payment for imports (i.e. buying the foreign currency spot before maturity). While legally permissable, such techniques fall under the window guidance of the authorities. When the yen is under downward pressure, as in 1979 and 1980, leading of import payments (or leading of export payments in times of yen strength) may be forbidden.

Export risk guarantees

Japan has a well-developed export guarantee programme to cover certain longer-term or soft currency risks where other hedging techniques are not extant. These programmes are offered through Export Import Bank of Japan and offer insurance to exporters against losses suffered when the currency in an export contract depreciates by more than a certain amount against the yen (in mid-1980 the trigger was 3%). Major OECD currencies are included and the insurance is applicable to contracts for the export of ships, aircraft, railroad stock and other heavy goods for up to 15 years.

Factoring

Where a Japanese exporter sells on open account and receives no bills eligible for discounting, it may assign the actual receivables as collateral for bank financing. Since foreign currency impact loans are readily available, this technique basically assists those exporters whose own credit is suspect and who cannot borrow fully on the basis of their balance sheet. If done through a commercial bank, rates are based on Euro-market ones; if done through the relatively new, but rapidly growing, factoring companies in Japan, somewhat higher costs may apply.

Leasing

An exporter in Japan, particularly in times of yen strength, may not be able to use yen invoicing nor wish to accept the weak currency of its importing customers. The exporter may consider selling its goods outright to a leasing company in the country of the importer, which leases them on to the ultimate user. (This is facilitated by the subsidiaries of Japanese leasing companies in S.E. Asian countries.) If other types of cover are unavailable or difficult, such leasing may be possible, but it requires a tripartite arrangement of considerable complexity.

INTERNAL METHODS

Internal methods to cover exchange exposure are often less costly, and sometimes less subject to official guidance, although the latter can never be excluded in Japan. These methods basically comprise asset-liability adjustments and include:

For present positions
— Prepayment of third-party commitments
— Intercompany maturity adjustments

For future expected positions
— Price adjustments
— Currency of billing changes
— Asset/liability structural changes
— Use of vehicle companies

Third party obligations

Basically a type of leading payment, this is permissible under foreign exchange control laws but subject to guidance by the government.

Intercompany

These underlie the same central government attitude, but prepayments here could be facilitated by changes in intercompany *terms*, so that faster flows into or out of Japan are achieved. Leading and lagging, despite official attempts at direction, are widely used in that country and are sometimes responsible for intensifying movements of the spot yen rate.

Price adjustments/currency of billing changes

These are standard methods of exporters world-wide. There is no official guidance in Japan as to the relation of price charged to currency movements and any currency can be used for billing.

Asset/liability management

Changing amounts and maturity structures of assets/liabilities in advance of rate change is an excellent anticipatory technique. Leading and lagging accomplishes this to some extent, as do re-scheduling of debt, changes in capitalisation, payment of dividends, etc. Where these adjustments cause cash to flow across Japan's borders, official attitudes towards external funds flows must be taken into account.

Vehicle companies

The use of vehicle companies can optimise exchange risk and liquidity management. Intermediary companies are usually located in a country with nominal exchange control and low rates of taxation, such as Switzerland or Bermuda. These are incorporated resident companies with a local board and set of accounts, whose major role typically is to buy the export products of the group and to reinvoice these for sale on to the ultimate customers. Credit terms, currency of invoicing and price to third party borrowers are unchanged.

Reinvoicing takes place either manually or by computer and the actual goods are shipped as before; thus the tariff/customs framework is unaffected. This is particularly important in multinational groupings with advantageous internal tariff regulations such as the European Economic Community.

The intermediary company may also buy from each exporting affiliate in its local currency and purchase for them their imports, reinvoicing back in local currency. If carried out rigorously, this puts all the trading exposure of the group into a central entity and creates a linkage of intercompany receivables. A Japanese-based corporation, therefore, could invoice exports to a reinvoicing company in yen and be invoiced in turn in yen for imports, thus moving yen exposure offshore to more flexible markets. By adjusting intercompany credit terms as well, exposed positions can be changed and liquidity augmented or drawn down as desired. A vehicle company creates more ties between subsidiaries, even where there is no direct trade between them, and materially increases the flexibility and range of exchange and liquidity management. The network of intercompany linkages thereby created is among the more powerful tools open to large, sophisticated companies—Japanese or otherwise—which have the initiative to create, and the understanding to operate successfully, such a company.

If arms-length pricing is maintained, the Japanese authorities cannot prevent the use of such vehicles. Many companies have created or are studying the inception of vehicles outside of Japan. Subsidiaries in Japan of multinational companies already utilising reinvoicing companies can be included.

THE TOKYO FOREIGN EXCHANGE MARKET

The Tokyo foreign exchange market exhibits the same type of government influence found in other financial markets in Japan. While moving towards a more modern structure and more interpenetration with the outside world, transactions are included in financial policy. An increasing range of currencies is available, longer maturities in the forward market are appearing and the market is benefiting from the slow internationalisation of the yen.

The Tokyo foreign exchange market before World War II had a small number of participants; the *zaibatsu* banks were dominant. Closed after the Japanese defeat, it re-opened again in July 1952. (In the interim, the occupying Allied powers controlled foreign exchange flows in Japan. All residents were required to sell foreign currencies received to the government through authorised banks.) With the reconstitution of the market, a group of "authorised foreign exchange" banks came again to be the primary dealers in foreign exchange.

Structure

The market structure includes the following participants:
— local brokers;
— Japanese banks;
— resident foreign bank branches;
— international brokers;
— Bank of Japan; and
— international institutions outside Japan.

Underlying these primary participants are Japan's great trading houses, other world-wide exporters/importers, and its overall trade, now over $200 billion equivalent annually.

Local brokers

The market is a broker system. A handful of firms—*tanshi*—form the Tokyo Foreign Exchange Brokers' Association, created in 1956, the principal intermediaries. The brokers are the nerve centre of a telephone market, with participant banks dealing with brokers for both sides on spot and forward deals. (A very limited market for foreign exchange exists in Osaka, but more than 99% of domestic deals in volume and number pass over Tokyo.) The *tanshi* are also the primary intermediaries in the local yen money markets, dealing in call, money, bills, certificates of deposit, and the Tokyo dollar "call" market. As such, they are at the heart of interbank deals of all kinds and of arbitrage between markets. However, the brokers are neutral in the foreign exchange trading area, despite being transmittors of government policy and carriers-out of tactics in domestic deals. They report large interbank deals immediately to Bank of Japan, so that the central bank can obtain a feeling for evolving rate trends. Senior officials of BOJ, upon retirement, may be placed in executive positions with the brokers' association on brokerage companies to maintain ties with and information flowing to the central bank.

Japanese banks

Participants include the city banks and the regional and local banks, but the former dominate; over 50% of volume pass over BOT and the city banks. These institutions deal on behalf of their major customers, for their own account and on behalf of BOJ when it is intervening. Customer business is highly attractive to commercial banks in Japan. Typically, the spread-over cost has been 100 basis points (1 yen per dollar) for normal trade transactions, based on the 10 a.m. "fixing", when a spot $/yen price is set for average transactions of the day. For large deals, however, major firms will insist on lower spreads: 50, 30 or even 20 basis points, but these are still profitable to banks compared to markets abroad. Furthermore, there is not the same shopping around for the best deals by corporations in Japan. Foreign exchange is seen as an important way to compensate a Japanese bank for its credit facilities and services. Foreign exchange business is usually allocated proportionately by firms to banks following the aggregate amounts of credit extended by each bank. If bank X extends to a company 10% of its total credit needs, then it will expect something around 10% of its foreign exchange business. (Conversely, if a foreign bank provides 1% of a Japanese company's lines, it will not get much more than 1% of exchange deals, no matter how sharp its quotes.)

The Japanese banks are eager for foreign exchange business, and it is not unheard of for them to offer a prime customer or solicitation bids at interbank, i.e. with no apparent spread. In fast-moving markets this can be risky; the rationale is to increase funds flowing through the bank in the thought that average deposits will also expand and to prove to Bank of Japan that emphasis is placed on customer service, rather than speculative position-taking.

Control of individual banks' dealing by the authorities is exerted by written and verbal reporting and by limits on open exchange positions. Each major resident bank in Japan calls the Bank of Japan daily to report what it is doing, which transactions have taken place and how the market looks. The central bank may require detailed information on which specific transactions have been consummated by which customers, enhancing the myriad information of a micro- and macro-nature which the authorities receive on economic and financial behaviour.

It is interesting that dealers in Japanese banks are rotated rather quickly. The position is not seen as a long-term one, but one of a sequence of jobs within a bank. Even adept traders can be moved on to other areas after a few years "on the board".

All banks, Japanese or foreign resident branches, are subject to net position limits in foreign exchange. The larger city banks may have net open limits of $30-50 million, the regional banks and foreign branches much smaller ones. These limits are raised from time to time, based on an unknown Bank of Japan formula; apparently it is related to the volume and percentage of customer transactions.

Resident foreign bank branches

Foreign branches, despite low open limits, play a larger role in the exchange markets than their diminutive status in domestic lending would imply. They are the Tokyo outposts of the world's largest, most able and most aggressive banks and their foreign parent and branch networks give them exceptional ability to trade, particularly outside the narrow, if dominant, band of dollar/yen. Many foreign banks have large dealing rooms with Western traders and modern technical paraphernalia. Because their swapped yen funding is closely related to foreign exchange, treasury functions overlap foreign exchange activities. Customer trading, for the relationship reasons explained above, plays only a small role compared to interbank and intrabank trading. But foreign banks have the ability to offer "exotic currencies", say, of the Middle East, and much longer-dated forwards; they also take important open positions in currencies other than the yen. Their competitive edge makes them account for over 10% of the Tokyo market; certain top foreign branches fall into the ten top trading entities in Tokyo of any nationality on a given day.

International brokers

Another international aspect of the market has come from the advent of international brokers. The first to open in Tokyo—Astley and Pearce—is still restricted from direct international dealing, despite hopes to create new links to outside markets. However, this is a portent of a more international market in Tokyo, complementing liberalisation in other areas.

Bank of Japan

Bank of Japan is a direct participant in the market when it intervenes to affect the value of the yen. BOJ traditionally operates only in the *spot* market, not in forward deals. It acts quietly through chosen Japanese city banks, but it is usually not hard to guess when the central bank is in the market. Not only are volumes higher *per se*, but also the very large deals offered by one bank on one single day are indicative. The usual deal in Tokyo is $1 million; when offers for a large multiple of that are made, say, $10 million, usually the central bank is present.

International institutions outside Japan

Through telephone and telex links, an appreciable volume of business is done with foreign-based institutions. Of daily volumes in Tokyo, as much as 20% may be accounted for by dealings with foreign head and branch offices of banks based in Tokyo or with correspondents which are not otherwise represented. Foreign banks may do up to 30% of their trading with foreign counterparties; in times of pressure for or against the yen, this area of trading then intensifies, representing speculative forces.

Trading Time, Rate Setting and Volumes

The stated interbank trading day in Tokyo runs from 9 a.m.-12 a.m. and from 1:30 p.m.-3:30 p.m.; at 3:30 p.m. each bank must be back within its net open position against the yen. The actual trading period is much wider; traders begin their day dealing with U.S. West Coast banks which are closing and extend it late into the evening with Southeast Asian and then European markets. The yen markets in a sense never close; they move from Tokyo, which starts the new day, to Hong Kong, to London, to New York, to San Francisco and then back to Tokyo.

The role of the Tokyo market as a yen rate-setter is disputed. Many observers feel that the yen is most protected in Tokyo proper and that here BOJ shows its hand as to the trend it hopes to induce. This is invalid, though, in the many times when the central bank is not intervening. More often than not, the market is left to commercial interests (trade and speculative); here a dominant factor is what the London and New York markets did when Tokyo traders were asleep. The Tokyo market often starts at the level where New York left off and moves in the same direction.[4]

Compared to volumes in other markets, the Tokyo market is still small. Dollar/yen trading volume has grown from a daily average of $100 million in 1976 to about $500 million in 1980 when intervention is not taking place. Even this volume is limited when compared with Japanese trade, where 1980 exports reached $120 billion, imports $115 billion and gross invisible and capital flows another $100 billion. Over $1 billion/day could thus be expected to be converted on average, since netting is not practised in Japan. The daily volume of $500 million is less than half of the flows which eventually get traded somewhere. And the majority of Tokyo deals, as elsewhere, are interbank, not trade-related. Thus the greater proportion of the country's exchange needs are not traded in its own markets, nor is it likely that the yen's value is set at home by domestic participants.

All the major convertible ones are traded, but these amount probably to no more than 5% in aggregate. As Japanese trade begins to be invoiced in other than dollars, this segment of the market should grow strongly, aided by the desire of bank participants to diversify their trading—particularly since currency X against currency Y positions, where neither is the yen, do not count against net open positions against the yen. The growing number of European branches and Western traders, and to a lesser extent, of Japanese bank branches abroad dealing with their head offices, increases the role of other currencies.

Maturities available in dollar/yen forward deals have lengthened. Two-year quotes are readily available at realistic rates and five-year quotes can be obtained, particularly if the commercial company can give a mandate to a single bank and wait a few days for the transaction to be done. Major trading houses, for example, may negotiate five-year forward deals (yen/dollar) with up to 60 consecutive monthly maturities to match expected receipts.

Interaction with Other Money Markets in Japan

The Tokyo foreign exchange market is closely linked with the Tokyo "dollar call market" and the short-term yen markets in Japan. The brokerage firms are the intermediary for all three participants. The Tokyo dollar call market, for example, is used to top up dollar funding requirements of resident banks or to lay off their very short-term dollar surpluses. It is possible to take dollars from that market for use in swap transactions, or to complete reverse swaps in the Tokyo market. Domestic yen deposit rates and Euro-yen rates can be out of line, allowing foreign exchange dealers to arbitrage between the two.

In summary, the Tokyo exchange market is somewhat smaller and more restricted than the trade flows of Japan might indicate. It is not necessarily the dominant area for trading in or setting the rate of its own currency. Bank participants have both strict open limits and scrutiny by the authorities. Despite these limitations, the Tokyo foreign exchange market adequately serves commercial demand and has the infrastructure and expertise to backstop a much larger Euro-currency market in Tokyo, if that desirable development is allowed to take place.

NOTES

1. A.R. Prindl. *Foreign Exchange Risk*, London: John Wiley Ltd., 1976.
2. Touche Ross. *Japan*, Tokyo: 1976, p. 90.
3. R.J. Ballon, Iwao Tomita and Hajime Usami. *Financial Reporting in Japan*, Tokyo: Kodansha International, 1976, pp. 251 ff.
4. See Mark Borsuk. "The Theory of Myopic Momentum", *Euromoney*, August 1980, pp. 91–102.

CHAPTER 13

Financial Management of Subsidiaries and Joint Ventures

Financial management of Western subsidiaries in Japan poses a number of problems less frequently encountered in similar entities in the U.S.A. and Europe. Some of these relate to market limitations and lack of instruments, others to differences in bank relationships. Also important are differences in perception of company goals, of financial targets, or even of the rationale behind, say, a joint venture. This chapter deals with the financial management problems in Japan which arise in subsidiaries or branches and are particularly strongly felt in joint ventures.

SUBSIDIARIES

Subsidiaries or branches in Japan fall under the profit framework and management guidelines of the foreign parent. They will be instructed to follow head office accounting and reporting practices and to accept the group's targets as their own.

These targets, however, may be more difficult for Japanese staff to perceive and considerable training and overseas contact may be needed to bring local staff to full understanding of the way treasury management (and related tax areas) are handled in the West. For that reason, the larger multinational subsidiaries in Japan in the oil, computer, automobile and office equipment fields all have Western finance managers. Even these persons can have problems with the compromise between doing things in Western or Japanese ways. A dichotomy of approach arises in the area of bank relationships, borrowing policy and foreign exchange coverage to protect parent interests, as well as head office reporting.

Bank Relationships

Chapter Seven discussed the psychology of Japanese financial officers when dealing with Japanese banks and the apparent scarring of such persons by the first "oil shock". Financial personnel in subsidiaries who have come from a

118

Japanese company background will often evince these characteristics. They will want to have close, warm and reliable ties with their banks. They will be willing to pay for those ties through large deposits maintained with, or other business sent to, their house banks; optimal treasury management will be of considerably less importance. They may feel a need to deal with many Japanese banks. Japanese financial staff think little of the time and expense which superfluous bank relationships imply, nor are they as prone to keep accurate records on cash balances and inherent costs to the company of compensating balances, in many cases.

Foreign financial managers will expect much different relations with banks. While respecting house bank relationships, they treat banks like any other suppliers and carefully assess the cost of bank services. Head offices will also not wish to overcompensate banks and may impose tight guidelines to squeeze value from deposits or other business, such as foreign exchange, channelled to financial institutions. They will have no respect for excess compensating balances nor much interest in the problems of the credit crunch of 1974/75. Head office treasurers will push for a zero balance posture, which, as Chapter Eleven showed, is possible to approach in Japan.

Japanese managers may then see their carefully nurtured relationships with domestic banks endangered, even disparaged, while U.S. managers will deplore money lying idle and banks being overcompensated. Further sources of friction here are that Western financial managers may feel happier dealing with Western banks and tend to turn to the foreign banking community in Tokyo or Osaka for assistance. They may wish to add Western banks while eliminating Japanese banks.

Head Office Reporting

The problems of accounting under two different systems can make the work of a financial manager difficult. Although Japanese accounting practice is loosely based on U.S. SEC accounting guidelines, more can be swept under the rug in Japan than in America. For example, the U.S. side must consolidate its equity share of a subsidiary owned 20–50%, while Japanese companies consolidate only proportionate income and then on a selective basis. Western headquarters will certainly ask for detailed financial statements: projections, forecasts, financial analysis, bank relationship reports, etc., which differ from those used by Japanese firms or which may not be required domestically.

Nowhere is this more telling than in the area of foreign exchange exposure management. An MNC subsidiary operating in Japan is a yen-based company. It faces the same problems of foreign exchange exposure as a Japanese company and will be concerned to protect yen assets and income against the vagaries of foreign exchange markets. The Western parent sees its consolidated Japanese net assets as exposed; this may be acceptable in some periods and decidedly risky in others. In 100% subsidiaries in Japan, manipulation of assets is used to reduce the yen exposure as recorded on the consolidated books of the overseas parent. Subsidiaries may be asked to borrow or repay yen loans. They may be asked to hedge portions of their balance sheet to fit in with overall corporate strategy abroad.

In a joint venture, these common techniques run counter to its yen basis. Acceleration or deceleration of payments may put the joint venture, as seen by the Japanese side, into a *more* risky position. Hedging transactions can be seen only to incur costs which are unnecessary for a yen-based entity. Borrowing or repayment of borrowings for exposure purposes have the same inherent problem.

Culture and Communications

There are many books on the subject of Japanese management and Japanese cultural differences. Suffice it to say that the Western manager dealing with Japanese colleagues can run into problems of this sort, which will add to the potential ones encountered in the technical areas above. He must realise that direct confrontation over differences of perception should be avoided. One must live with the Japanese concept of the *ringi*, in which each member of a team has a chance to give an opinion and ultimately is involved in the decision-making process, whether or not he knows much about the matter. This may irritate the Western manager, who sees time spent discussing apparently simple problems as wasted. These problems are accentuated in the joint venture, as shown below.

JOINT VENTURES

The financial landscape in Japan is littered with the wrecks of joint ventures (JVs) which have failed. Even such household names in the West as J.P. Stevens, Gillette and Kraft Cheese have seen their Japanese partnerships turn sour or go bankrupt.

Obviously, there are almost as many reasons for joint venture failures as failed joint ventures: poor market analysis, misreading of trends, production cost problems and many similar non-financial obstacles to profitable growth. The financial management of JVs is, however, in itself a highly complicated area, which throws up a further range of complications unseen in branches or affiliates. Successful fielding of such financial difficulties can add much to the viability of a joint venture; mishandling will add to the problems which in the aggregate have often led to failure of such companies.

The Growth of JVs in Japan

Japan has a plethora of JVs and new ones continue to be founded. Two reasons lie behind this: the Japanese prohibition against 100% direct investment by most foreign companies during much of the post-war period and the complexities of entering the Japanese marketplace and dealing with its distribution system.

The Japanese governmental/industrial/financial tie-up exists in large part to promote and to protect Japanese interests. One way to encourage Japanese rebuilding in a wide range of industries after the devastation of World War II was to prohibit the entry of foreign companies wishing to manufacture in its potentially large market. Even distribution/sales companies owned by non-residents posed a considerable threat, firstly to local producers and secondly to the nation's exchange reserves, if imports rapidly increased as a result.

The Foreign Investment Law was passed in 1949 and remained in force until 1979. Its constraints basically required MITI or MOF approval for 100% direct investment in most industries; investment in other industries was prohibited from the beginning. MITI/MOF approvals, of course, were seldom given, except in scattered cases, usually related to the reconstruction of companies already here before the war, or in critical industries of high technology which Japan could not hope to emulate quickly (e.g. computers).

The only way then to enter the Japan market was through exports or creation of a joint venture with a Japanese partner. To export usually meant putting one's business in the hands of local agents or trading firms, where neither enthusiasm or price maintenance could be assured. (Exporting directly also meant going through the thicket of invisible barriers, controls, quotas and inspections, about which acrimonious debate is still going on.) A JV with a good Japanese partner could in theory offset these problems. Joint ventures were more or less readily allowed in industrial and marketing areas. The JV structure, where the Japanese side was a large, capable firm, offered immediately tappable expertise in the form of market knowledge and distribution. Production could be facilitated, or left to the Japanese side on a licensing basis. Dealing with the government would be handled by existing officials of the JV partner, already well-versed in such negotiations. Requisite permissions would be eased, access to Japanese banks and financing increased.

Seeking these theoretical advantages, a large number of Western multinational companies came to Tokyo in the form of 50/50 JVs (or in other partnerships where they owned less than 50% of the equity). Table 13.1 shows the number of JVs formed in the period 1966/78, including such Western companies as Caterpillar, General Electric, General Motors, ICI and Ciba Geigy and the amounts invested in JVs in the period 1948/78.

Financial Management Choices

Regardless of the type of product produced or sold, clear choices have to be made as to the financial management of joint ventures. As one alternative, all financial matters can be left to the Japanese side. If the JV is small and has few Westerners, this is an obvious route to follow. In companies large enough to allow specialists to be sent from the Western parent, the finance manager might be foreign, particularly when the Japanese side is basically a domestic partner or more interested in acquiring technology than in the bottom line.

Table 13.1
Joint Venture Establishment in Japan, 1948/78
(US $1,000)

FY	No. of JVs	Amount invested
1948/53	N.a.	28,847
1954/59	N.a.	62,494
1960/65	N.a.	180,735
1966	142	39,812
1967	169	29,778
1968	194	52,701
1969	300	53,776
1970	455	114,489
1971	445	255,463
1972	747	160,431
1973	756	167,268
1974	655	153,715
1975	615	166,503
1976	652	195,688
1977	693	224,473
1978	705	235,494

Source: *Annual Review 1979*, published by International Finance Bureau, Ministry of Finance

In the largest JV companies, financial staff from both sides are seconded to make up the treasury division in Japan.

Whichever of these alternatives is chosen—and the choice is usually made from the point of view of convenience or cost, rather than logic—shapes the financial path of the JV. Financing decisions, foreign exchange hedging decisions, cash management practices—all can lead in directions not originally envisioned, or necessarily desired, by one or both partners. These choices arising from different management styles may bring friction between the partners.

Potential Conflicts

Different perceptions: a case history

Joint ventures, at inception, are usually based on a Joint Venture Agreement and Articles of Association, often complemented by side agreements concerning production, licensing fees, royalties, etc. Financial management is typically not spelled out, being considered, if at all, a passive response to financial problems encountered in the course of the partnership. But financial management is predicated on *perceptions*: perceptions of risk, of profit opportunities, of the ultimate goals of the venture. Such ultimate goals as market penetration or return on assets, while sometimes given lip-service in the JV Agreement, may vary appreciably between the two partners.

A classic case is that of a joint venture in the food industry. The partners are Japanese and European; both ranked within *Fortune's* top 500 multinationals in 1980. This joint venture was formed to manufacture consumer products in the Japanese market and take over previous European imports to Japan. The European side wanted to expand their local sales in the world's second largest market for their particular line of goods and felt it necessary to link up with a Japanese partner with strong production and distribution capabilities. Their primary goal, of course, was to produce appreciable levels of profitability within a reasonable period of time after start-up.

The Japanese side's target was apparently different. Throughout the course of several years, it became clear that they were primarily interested in learning the marketing techniques of the European company and some of its production methods. Return on assets was of less concern. Furthermore, the Japanese side was strongly committed to diversification from its traditional industrial base, which was stagnant and slowly dying.

A number of conflicts arose from those differences of perception of the purpose of the subsidiary. The most important was in marketing. The Japanese side proved not to have enough access to the food distribution channels necessary for self-sustained growth of sales and thus only expensive advertising had a chance of introducing the JV's European products throughout Japan. The European partner, well-experienced in advertising, saw this as the crux of success in the food industry and was committed to spending large sums of money for the first several years of the joint venture to make its name and products well-known. It was prepared to finance these losses by local borrowings and further infusion of capital if necessary, given long-range prospects of future success. Over time, the diversification plans of the Japanese parent were not singularly successful and it began to oppose the introduction of new products, expansion of production machinery and anything but the most minimal advertising. An edict came from the president of the Japanese partner that all subsidiaries and joint ventures of that company must show profitable sales results. Given a very low market share and reduced Japanese growth rates in the late 1970s, the joint venture's sales never really got off the ground. Marketing was cut to the bone, so that a nominal profit could be shown annually. The subsidiary, at the point of writing, languishes and is unlikely to have much future growth.

Both parents are disappointed. The European side has not had the market penetration which it wanted and has lost its share of capital three times over. (It probably chose the wrong partner, whose weak distribution structure hindered the joint venture as much as its intransigence in bearing the marketing expense.) It will likely have to wind up the subsidiary or buy out the Japanese side, either of which will cost several million dollars to restore accumulated past losses. The Japanese parent, too, is disappointed. Its efforts to diversify remain unsuccessful and it is tarred with another failure of a joint venture bearing its name. It, too, faces very large payments for funding the accumulated past losses whenever the joint venture structure is changed; it has learned little about marketing techniques or production methods, as marketing was never allowed to develop a full European sway in Japan. The moral again is that two partners may have quite different perceptions about the purpose of the joint venture and thus about the way in which it should be managed.

Different profit motivations

In the above case, different long-term goals were clearly the main internal problem the subsidiary faced, but more fundamental differences between the Japanese way and the Western way of looking at things also lead to potential internal conflicts. For example, Westerners, whose companies are publicly owned, scrutinised by security analysts, bought or sold by institutions and subject to strict accounting disclosure laws, are quite concerned about not only profit, but also about a well-known series of ratios such as return on assets, return on sales or return on equity. Trends in these ratios are widely watched and companies try to show improvement not only in the gross amount of sales but also in the basic profitability of their endeavours. Japanese companies are often held by a tight group of stockholders and have close relationships with large institutional holders, particularly with house banks. There is less pressure for them to show ever-increasing profit growth or returns on assets. Disclosure laws are weaker in Japan; joint ventures do not have to disclose anything publicly, nor do the Japanese partners consolidate their share of joint ventures in the way most Western accounting practices require. More important to the Japanese way of thinking is growth in market share, maintenance of reputation, maintenance of employee stability and employment itself, for which paternalistic concern is evidenced. The joint venture whose Western managers strongly push profit and return on sales at the potential expense of labour relations, bank relations or other Japanese traditional practices, will certainly come into conflict with Japanese managers of the firm.

Conflicting reporting systems

The joint venture faces the same problems in reporting systems and exchange exposure management as does the subsidiary, intensified by the differing yen and foreign currency bias from which the two parents look at its positions.

There are, however, a number of highly successful joint ventures; the following describes one of the better-known cases.

Caterpillar Mitsubishi as Example of a Successful Joint Venture

This is the largest joint venture in Japan, founded in November 1963 between Mitsubishi Heavy Industries, a leading Japanese shipbuilder and heavy equipment manufacturer, and Caterpillar Tractor Company to produce the wide range of construction equipment of the Caterpillar Group. At the time of establishment, this industry was rather moribund in Japan; the introduction of a strong new company has, over the past ten years, revitalised the whole area, including other local competitors such as Komatsu. The joint venture now has an annual sales volume of over $1 billion and exports strongly throughout Asia.

Despite the implicit problems which Caterpillar Mitsubishi could have in, for example, exchange exposure, the company has developed an excellent approach to financial management. This is handled jointly; Caterpillar, which provides top management, marketing management, and production control, also furnishes two financial executives from abroad on a permanent, rotating basis. The more senior of these executives is responsible for financial, accounting and tax matters and all managers in those departments report to him. Day-to-day banking and treasury problems are handled by two managers, one American and one Japanese. They split their responsibilities equally so that, roughly, foreign-related transactions, i.e., export finance, foreign exchange cover and dealings with multinational banks, are handled by the American side, and domestic receipts and funding from Japanese banks are handled by Japanese. Not only does this use the corporate experience and language abilities of both individuals, but it also focuses their knowledge towards the areas which specifically affect their parent companies. Since working capital and trade financing is split between domestic and foreign banks, this division of responsibility leaves considerable scope to both manager groups, whose staff are carefully chosen for their flexibility.

Foreign exchange exposure is handled jointly and potential conflicts here are mitigated by treating the joint venture as a Japanese company. Financial officers' first responsibility is to Caterpillar Mitsubishi. Foreign exchange risks are covered when they affect the local subsidiary's financial statements, not by it on behalf of Peoria. The U.S. parent, therefore, covers its consolidated exposure in the joint venture separately. There is considerable travel between Peoria and Tokyo and Japanese financial staff are often in the U.S. Communications thereby established show the Japanese side why the U.S. parent may require information beyond that requested in Japan and show the U.S. side the different nature of its JV as opposed to a fully-owned plant. This company appears to have supplemented its excellent production and marketing success with outstanding working relations between the financial executives of both sides.

GUIDELINES FOR SUCCESSFUL FINANCIAL MANAGEMENT OF A FOREIGN COMPANY

Delineation of responsibilities

No matter which approach is taken to financial management decision-making, delineation of responsibility of both Western and Japanese managers is critical. Job specifications should be written down and a form of tracking the responsibilities and decisions of managers instituted.

Clear exposition of goals

This relates to communications. Problems arise when either side feels that other managers are doing a poor job or do not understand the techniques and approaches of the partner. Ways to iterate these goals and techniques and to review progress towards achieving them should be established.

Explanation of constraints

It is often hard for financial executives to understand the different accounting and reporting procedures of the other partner. There has to be full explanation of the differences between Japanese practice and the accounting systems of the Western partner. Normally, the Western partner will also require more detailed reporting information, and the need for and use of that data must be explained. Corporate guidelines regarding financial strategy are a similar area for review.

Travel

It is important that the Japanese financial managers travel to the home office of the parent so that better understanding of all the above can be achieved. It is also clearly useful when the U.S. or European financial director comes to Japan for him to work with the joint venture. This should be repeated on an annual basis if possible.

Job exchange

Some joint ventures have sent Japanese staff to work at Head Office for a number of years. When they come back, they can report to both sides of the company with fuller understanding. Switching of jobs within the joint venture between Western and Japanese members can achieve much of the same purpose.

In conclusion, financial management for a foreign company, particularly with a Japanese partner, is tricky enough if one had to deal only with differences in exchange control, banking markets, legal constraints and floating rates. When potential misunderstandings from different perceptions, goals and guidelines are added to this list, considerable disruption to smooth operation can appear. It is not surprising that the companies which are best at solving the joint venture problems of marketing and production are often those which have solved the equally difficult job of joint financial management.

CHAPTER 14

Summary

This volume has attempted to describe the structure of the Japanese financial system and how it is directed. An emphasis has been to explain the apparent rigidity of the system by looking at the Japanese perception of their economic status. Considerable weight was put on the thesis that the Japanese belief in their economic fragility, as compared to rival trading nations, is an important factor in the ways the monetary system has developed and monetary control instruments are chosen. It has pointed out that a country which concentrates on its fragility—real or not—and which does not perceive a major external financial role for itself, will tend to form a closed circle and control its banking system by strict rules and guidance. Government becomes the force preserving and protecting the system, since the economy is believed not able to face the slings and arrows of external events without protection. This is particularly true of the financial system, where it is presumed that malevolent forces may not be further than a telex wire away.

National perceptions of Japan's strength in part explain what appears to be an unnecessary degree of control by the Ministry of Finance and the Bank of Japan over a strong economy and a rapidly maturing banking sector. They explain, too, much of the reluctance to allow supply and demand to allocate capital, the yen to play a larger role in world economic affairs or Tokyo to grow into a London-type market.

Whether or not the Japanese perception is correct does not in the first instance matter. Beliefs as well as concrete facts can shape government attitudes and measures. Indeed, if the author's contention that a feeling of fragility is a national one is correct, then strict government controls will be all the more accepted by participants in the economy and the financial markets. Historical patterns of obedience to authority and maintenance of group cohesion further support the role of government.

Minute direction of the financial system and its component parts is also in part necessitated by the relatively few money market instruments available. Indirect techniques, such as those used by the Federal Reserve System in the U.S., are less appropriate in a country where reserve requirements are so far immaterial and rates of interest are set artificially. Government indirect action to affect supply and demand for funds would not now be as successful in Japan as direct allocation of fund flows and interest rate-setting have been.

Western economists see such direct controls and the manpower requirement they imply as inefficient. They also question whether government officials, no matter how skilled, can guide such a large and mature economy as well as it would guide itself by the collective decisions of profit-seeking institutions.

The Japanese themselves are asking precisely these questions. They realise how costly and irksome government regulation and direction are. Western ways of fostering economic growth and directing the financial system are well-known in Japan, and constantly scrutinised. The endemic failures of U.S. and European countries in the past decade, however, do not give them overwhelming reasons to change what has until recently been a demonstrably successful system.

As shown above, institutional lag may also be a reason that the monetary system is not as modern as the industrial base. More freedom in domestic markets, and complete freedom in a newly-created offshore one, would be natural counterparts of an economy perceived as mature and possibly heading for post-industrial status. But institutional ways of controlling the system, including delineation of now unnecessary sectoral boundaries, remain those used in earlier stages of economic growth. The "safety-net" feature of the Japanese system: the certainty that a major Japanese financial institution will not be allowed to fail, is another factor in delaying change. Some—perhaps many—bankers may not wish to change the controlled nature of their industry and expose themselves more fully to the winds of competition and greater risks of failure.

Yet, chances are that the national debate on these issues will result in considerably freer markets at home and offshore. The sharp distinctions between banking sectors, and between commercial banking and securities houses, are breaking down. Clear trends towards fuller-scale, if not universal, banking have been identified. Some new money market instruments, including a wider range of Treasury bills and yen certificates of deposit, have been created; repurchase arrangements have been sanctioned and offer market rather than administered rates of interest. The Bank of Japan's official policy is to continue and deepen trends towards domestic liberalisàtion.

Exchange control has been altered from a negative system of prior authorisation to a positive system allowing most transactions to flow in or out of Japan freely. Whether this step will be as great a change as, say, the scrapping of U.K. exchange control or whether the older ways of influencing transactions by prior direction and prohibition will linger on is yet to be tested. Substantial escape clauses have been left in to limit the new freedoms if market chaos threatens Japan; unsettled markets are certain to reappear regularly in the future, and the legal aspects of official control are minor in any case compared to the other authority vested in the Ministry of Finance or the Bank of Japan. But the change is a symbolic one and a step in the direction of more freedom.

The yen itself continually grows in international usage. The yen's 13%

portion of the reconstructed Special Drawing Rights, the use of yen samurai bonds and yen private placements by foreign borrowers and especially its holding in international reserves are forcing it into international status, despite concerns these trends raise in the minds of the authorities. Such major developments as the surge of OPEC countries' official investments in yen securities are a two-edged blessing; highly welcome in 1980 as an offset to a deficit current account, the resultant increased internationalisation of the yen runs counter to the traditional nature of state control of currency and its uses. However, these trends now appear irreversible.

The last of the major areas of liberalisation—the creation of an offshore Euro-dollar market—is yet to come. No progress towards establishing such a market can be noted; the introduction of reserve requirements on deposits from abroad even acts in the opposite direction as yet another impediment. Yet, within the decade of the 1980s one can with some confidence predict that the technical barriers to such a market will have been abolished or waived for truly "out-out" transactions, giving Tokyo an opportunity to grow into its proper status as one of the world's three great financial centres. The invisible income arising therefrom should develop to the levels of the City of London over time and the other Asian Euro-dollar centres may correspondingly suffer. Negative effects of such a market can be kept away from domestic areas by the same type of controls now used by the Bank of England.

In the meantime, the domestic yen markets offer a new and increasing pool of capital to be tapped by foreign borrowers. While access to that pool is still predicated on the position of the Japanese Balance of Payments, samurai bonds and yen loans abroad should be available for the benefit of government and some corporate borrowers.

For managers of local subsidiaries in Japan, using the banking market raises unique problems of banking relationships and cultural differences. The limits of, and controls upon, financial institutions and media make the task of treasury management more complex than in, say, European countries with different financial systems. Yet cash management systems in Japan are excellent, and effective use of surplus funds is becoming more possible. Western financial management techniques, used to manage cash flows, improve yields on surplus funds or to hedge foreign exchange exposure, are increasingly available or adaptable to Japanese conditions. Understanding the perceptions of Japanese negotiating partners: the regulatory authorities, banks or one's own employees, is the critical factor in successfully implementing those techniques and getting them accepted.

Although the text points out some anomalies in the Japanese banking system, the author does not intend to be overly critical of a country whose success is self-evident. Japan's great manufacturing and trading houses would not have brought it to the world's second largest Gross National Product if they were not backstopped and supported by an adequate financial system, inefficient and static as it now seems in certain respects. And those inefficiencies will likely be weeded out sooner rather than later, if the Japanese approach the modernisation of the financial system with their customary strength and sense of purpose. The financial system is the subject of considerable national debate at a number of levels. While the importance of consensus in Japan means that major changes in, say, the financial area will be deliberated at great length, it also means that change is rapidly implemented, once agreed.

Selected Bibliography

1. *General/Cultural*

Benedict, Ruth, *The chrysanthemum and the sword: patterns of Japanese culture*, New York: The World Publishing Co., 1967.

Brzezinski, Zbigniew, *The fragile blossom: crisis and change in Japan*, New York: Harper and Row, 1972.

Cleaver, Charles G., *Japanese and Americans: Cultural Parallels and Paradoxes*, Minneapolis, Minn.: University of Minnesota Press, 1976.

Doi, Takeo, *The Anatomy of Dependence*, Tokyo: Kodansha, 1971.

Forbis, William H., *Japan today: people, places, power*, Tokyo: Charles E. Tuttle Co. Inc., 1976.

Gibney, Frank, *Five gentlemen of Japan: the portrait of a nation's character*, Tokyo: Charles E. Tuttle Co. Inc., 1973.

Gibney, Frank, *Japan: the fragile superpower*, Tokyo: Charles E. Tuttle Co. Inc., 1975.

Hearn, Lafcadio, *Japan: an attempt at interpretation*, New York: Macmillan, 1904.

Nakane, Chie, *Human relations in Japan*, Tokyo: Ministry of Foreign Affairs, 1972.

Nakane, Chie, *Kinship and economic organisation in rural Japan*, London: Athlone Press, University of London, 1967.

Nakane, Chie, *Japanese Society*, Berkeley and Los Angeles, Calif.: University of California Press, 1972.

Rabinowitz, Richard W., "Law and the social process in Japan", *Transactions of the Asiatic Society of Japan*, X, Third Series, 1968.

Reischauer, Edwin O., *Japan: the story of a nation*, Tokyo: Charles E. Tuttle Co. Inc., 1971.

Reischauer, Edwin O., *The Japanese*, Cambridge, Mass.: Harvard University Press, 1977.

Sansom, G.B., *The Western World and Japan*, New York: Alfred Knopf, 1950.

Singer, Kurt, *Mirror, Sword and Jewel*, New York: George Braziller, 1973.

Vogel, Ezra, F., *Japan as number one: lessons for America*, Cambridge, Mass.: Harvard University Press, 1979.

2. *Economic Development*

Denison, Edward F. and Chung, William K., *How Japan's economy grew so fast: the sources of postwar expansion*, Washington, D.C.: Brookings Institution, 1976.

Lippit, Victor D., "Economic development in Meiji Japan and contemporary China: a comparative study", *Cambridge Journal of Economics*, 2, 1978.

Lockwood, William W., *The Economic Development of Japan*, Princeton, N.J.: Princeton University Press, 1954.

Nakamura, James I., *Agricultural production and the economic development of Japan 1873–1922*, Princeton, N.J.: Princeton University Press, 1966.

Roberts, John G., *Mitsui: three centuries of Japanese business*, New York: John Weatherhill Inc., 1973.

Tsurumi, Shigeto, *The mainsprings of Japanese growth: a turning point?*, Paris: Atlantic Institute for International Affairs, Atlantic Papers, March 1976.

Yamamura, Kozo, "A Study of Samurai Income and Entrepreneurship", *Quantitative Analyses of Economic and Social Aspects of the Samurai in Tokugawa and Meiji Japan*, Cambridge, Mass.: Harvard University Press, 1974.

Yamamura, Kozo, "Economic responsiveness in Japanese industrialization", *Business enterprise and economic change*, ed. L.P. Cain and P.J. Uselding, Kent, Ohio: Kent State University Press, 1973.

Yamamura, Kozo, "Then came the great depression: Japan's interwar years", *The great depression revisited*, H. Van der Wee (ed.), Amsterdam: Martinus Nijhoff, 1973.

Yamamura, Kozo, "Toward a reexamination of the economic history of Tokugawa Japan, 1600–1867", *Journal of Economic History*, *XXXIII*, (3), September 1973.

3. *Japanese Economy*

Abegglen, James C. and Hout, Thomas M., "Facing up to the trade gap with Japan", *Foreign Affairs*, *57*, (1), Fall 1978.

Ballon, Robert J. and Lee, Eugene H. (eds.), *Foreign investment and Japan*, Tokyo: Sophia University, 1972.

Hanabusa, Masamichi, *Trade problems between Japan and Western Europe*, Farnborough: Saxon House, 1979.

Ho, Alfred K., *Japan's trade liberalization in the 1960s*, New York: International Arts and Sciences Press Inc., 1973.

Kahn, Herman, *The emerging Japanese superstate*, Harmondsworth: Penguin Books Ltd., 1973.

Kahn, Herman and Pepper, Thomas, *The Japanese Challenge*, London: Harper and Row, 1978.

Ministry of International Trade and Industry, *Japan's Industrial Structure—A Long Range Vision*, Tokyo: 1978.

Ministry of International trade and Industry, *Japan Reporting—The Japanese Post-war Industrial Society: its Development and its Characteristics*, Tokyo: 1979.

Patrick, Hugh and Rosovsky, Henry (eds.), *Asia's New Giant: How the Japanese Economy Works*, Washington, D.C., Brookings Institution, 1976.

4. *Development of the Financial System*

Adams, T.F.M. and Hoshii, Iwao, *A financial history of the new Japan*, Tokyo: Kodansha International Ltd., 1972.

Burke, William, "Japan's entrance into the international financial community", *American Journal of Economics and Sociology*, *23*, (3), July 1964.

Crawcour, E.S., "Changes in Japanese commerce in the Tokugawa period", *Journal of Asian Studies*, *22*, (4), August 1963.

Crawcour, E.S., "The development of a credit system in seventeenth-century Japan", *Journal of Economic History*, *XXI*, (3), 1961.

Crawcour, E.S. and Yamamura, Kozo, "The Tokugawa monetary system: 1787–1868", *Economic Development and Cultural Change*, *18*, (4), July 1970.

Fuji Bank, *The Fuji Bank*, 1880–1980, Tokyo: 1980.

Japan Business History Institute (ed.), *The Mitsui Bank: a history of the first 100 years*, Tokyo: Mitsui Bank Ltd., July 1976.

Patrick, Hugh T., "Japan 1864–1914", *Banking in the early stages of industrialization*, R. Cameron (ed.), Oxford: Oxford University Press, 1967.

Tokyo Metropolitan Government (ed.), *Financial history of Tokyo: a century of growth amid change*, Tokyo: Tokyo Metropolitan Government, December 1972.

Yamamura, Kozo, "Japan 1868–1930: a revised view", *Banking and economic development*, R. Cameron (ed.), Oxford: Oxford University Press, 1972.

5. *Present Financial Structure*

Bank of Japan, *The Japanese Financial System*, Tokyo: 1978.

Bank of Japan, *Outline of the Functions of the Business Department*, Tokyo: n.d.

Federation of Bankers Associations of Japan, *Banking System in Japan*, Tokyo: 1979.

Fuji Bank, Limited, *Guidebook on Banking Services in Japan*, Tokyo: 1979.

Fujioka, Masao, *Japan's international finance: today and tomorrow*, Tokyo: *The Japan Times* Ltd., 1979.

Gillan, J.P., "Banking Practices in Japan", *The Journal of the ACCJ*, December 1977/January 1978.

Kuroda, Iwao and Oritani, Yoshiharu, "A reexamination of the unique features of Japan's corporate financial structure", *Japanese Economic Studies*, VIII, (4), Summer 1980.

Mitsubishi Trust and Banking Corporation, "Interest Rate Determination in Japan", *Mitsubishi Trust Report*, July 1978.

Monroe, Wilbur F., *Japan: financial markets and the world economy*, New York: Praeger Publishers Inc., 1973.

Pressnell, L.S. (ed.), *Money and banking in Japan*, London: Macmillan Press Ltd., 1973.

Suzuki, Yoshio, *Money and banking in contemporary Japan*, New Haven, Conn.: Yale University Press, 1980.

Trust Company Association of Japan, *Trust Banks in Japan 1980*, Tokyo: 1980.

Wallich, Henry C. and Mable I., "Banking and Finance" in Patrick, Hugh and Rosovsky, Henry (eds.), *Asia's New Giant: How the Japanese Economy Works*, Washington, D.C.: Brookings Institution, 1976.

Weiss, Martin D., "Japan Review: Capital Flows and the Monetarist Model", *Asian Banking*, December 1980.

Yamane Tanshi Company, *Money Market in Japan and Tanshi companies*, Tokyo: Yamane, 1977.

6. Bond Market

Bennett, John B. and Doelling, Norman, *Investing in Japanese securities*, Tokyo: Charles E. Tuttle, 1972.

Daiwa Securities Co. Ltd., *Introduction to Japanese Bonds*, Tokyo, 1979.

Industrial Bank of Japan Ltd. (ed.), *Handbook of the Japanese bond market 1979*, Tokyo: Institute for Financial Affairs, Inc., 1979.

Nomura Securities Co., Ltd., *An Introduction to the Japanese Bond Market*, Tokyo: 1978.

Securities Public Information Center of Japan, "Japan's Securities Market 1980", Tokyo: S.P.I.C.J., 1979.

Tatsuta, Misao, *Securities regulation in Japan*, Tokyo: University of Tokyo Press, 1970.

7. Regulatory/Governmental Background

Bank of Japan, *The Bank of Japan, its Organization and Monetary Policies*, Tokyo: 1973.

Campbell, John Creighton, *Contemporary Japanese Budget Politics*, Berkeley, Calif.: University of California Press, 1977.

Johnson, Chalmers, Japan: *Public Policy Companies*, Washington, D.C.: American Enterprise Institute for Public Policy Research, 1978.

Komiya, Ryutaro and Yamamoto, Kozo, "The Officer in charge of Economic Affairs in the Japanese Government", paper presented at the Conference on the Role of the Economist in the Government, Dubrovnik, Jugoslavia, March 1979.

Murakami, Hyoe and Hirschmeier, Johannes (eds.), *Politics and Economics in Contemporary Japan*, Tokyo: Japan Culture Institute, 1979.

Nakane, Fukio (trans. and ed.), *Japanese Laws relating to Banks*, Tokyo: Eibun-Horei-Sha, Inc., 1977.

Rimbara, Yukio and Santomero, Anthony M., "A study of credit rationing in Japan", *International Economic Review*, *17*, (3), October 1976.

134

Spaulding, Robert M., Jr., *Imperial Japan's higher civil service examinations*, Princeton, N.J.: Princeton University Press, 1967.

Stockwin, J.A.A., Japan: *Divided Politics in a Growth Economy*, New York: Norton, 1975.

Watanabe, Akio, "Foreign policy making, Japanese style", *International Affairs, 54*, (1), January 1978.

Yanaga, Chitoshi, *Big Business in Japanese Politics*, New Haven, Conn.: Yale University Press, 1968.

8. *Business Organisation and Finance*

Abegglen, James C., "Why Many Fail in Japan", Tokyo: Boston Consulting Group, n.d.

Caves, Richard E. and Uekusa, Masu, *Industrial organisation in Japan*, Washington, D.C.: Brookings Institution, 1976.

De Mente, Boye, *Japanese manners and ethics in business*, Tokyo: East Asia Publishing Co. Ltd., 1960.

Drucker, Peter J., "Behind Japan's Success", *Harvard Business Review*, January/February 1981.

Drucker, Peter J., "What we can learn from Japanese Management", *Harvard Business Review*, March/April 1971.

Hattori, Ichiro, "Corporate structure and decision making in Japan", *Sophia University Socio-Economic Institute: International Management Development Seminars*, Bulletin No. 65, 1977.

Japan External Trade Organization (JETRO), *Financial and Labour Practices in Japan*, Tokyo: 1974.

Kobayashi, Noritake, "The Japanese approach to multinationalism", *Journal of World Trade Law, 10*, (2), March/April 1976.

Kojima, Kiyoshi, *Japanese direct foreign investment: a model of multinational business operations*, Tokyo: Charles E. Tuttle Co. Inc., 1979.

Marubeni Corporation, *The unique world of the Sogo Shosha*, Tokyo: 1978.

Norbury, Paul and Bownas, Geoffrey (eds.), *Business in Japan*, London: Macmillan Press Ltd., 1974.

Ozawa, Terutomo, "Japan's multinational enterprise: the political economy of outward dependency", *World Politics*, December 1978.

Ozawa, Terutomo, "Peculiarities of Japan's multinationalism: facts and theories, *Quarterly Review of the Banca Nazionale del Lavoro*, (115), December 1975.

Vogel, Ezra (ed.), *Modern Japanese Organization and Decision Making*, Berkeley, Calif.: University of California Press, 1975.

Yamazaki, Kiyoshi; Kobayashi, Noritake and Doi, Teruo, "Toward Japanese-type multinational corporations", *Japanese Economic Studies*, Summer 1977.

Yoshino, M.Y., *Japan's managerial system: tradition and innovation*, Cambridge, Mass.: Massachusetts Institute of Technology Press, 1971.

Yoshino, M.Y., *Japan's Multinational Enterprises*, Cambridge, Mass.: Harvard University Press, 1976.

9. *Accounting*

Ballon, Robert J.; Tomito, Iwao and Usami, Hajime, *Financial reporting in Japan*, Tokyo: Kodansha International Ltd., 1976.

Deloitte Haskins and Sells, *Taxation in Japan*, New York: 1979.

Price Waterhouse & Co., *Doing Business in Japan*, Tokyo: 1975.

Touche Ross International, *Japan*, New York: 1976.

Index